COMBAT AIRCRAFT

A-10

CRESCENT BOOKS
New York

A Salamander Book

This edition © Salamander Books Ltd., 1992

This 1992 edition published by
Crescent Books,
distributed by Outlet Book Company, Inc.,
a Random House Company,
225 Park Avenue South,
New York, New York 10003.

Printed and Bound in Hong Kong

ISBN 0 517 06738 2

8 7 6 5 4 3 2 1

All correspondence concerning the content
of this volume should be addressed to
Salamander Books Ltd.

Contents

Development	4
Structure	16
Powerplant	28
Weapons and Avionics	34
Deployment	46
Performance and Tactics	52
Glossary and Abbreviations	64

Acknowledgements

The author and editor would like to thank all
those who have contributed information and
pictures to this book. Photograph sources are
credited individually at the end of the book,
but particular thanks are due to George
Thune, Bill Lowenstein and Dave Wright of
Fairchild Republic Company.

The following works were consulted in the
course of preparing this book:
Flight International, particularly the
24 January 1976 issue
Air Force Magazine, particularly the
July 1983 issue
*Aviation Week and Space Technology,
Defense Week*, May 31, 1983
International Defense Review, 2/79
Bill Gunston, *Attack Aircraft of the West*,
Ian Allan 1974
Doug Richardson, *Aviation Fact File – F-16*,
Salamander 1983
Freidrich Wiener, *The Armies of the Warsaw
Pact Nations*, Carl Ueberreuter 1981

Authors

Between 1973 and 1979, Bill Sweetman was
on the staff of *Flight International*, where as
well as covering the air transport industry
he launched the 'Flight Intelligence' series
of detailed technical analyses of modern
Soviet military aircraft. From 1979 to 1981 he
was Air Correspondent of the British
national Sunday newspaper, *The Observer*.
He has contributed to the Washington-
based *Defense Week*, in addition to
Interavia and *International Defense Review*.

Lindsay Peacock
Author of the 1992 updated edition, Lindsay
Peacock has been a freelance aviation
writer and photcgrapher since 1976. He is
the author of several hundred magazine
articles and a number of books including
Salamander's *Strike Aces* (1989).

Credits

Project Manager: Ray Bonds

Editors: Bernard Fitzsimons, Tony Hall

Designed by Grub Street Design, London. This edition adapted by Studio Gossett

Jacket: Kai Choi

Colour profile below:
Terry Hadler

Diagrams: TIGA

Three-view drawings and colour profiles:
© Pilot Press

Cutaway drawing and A2D-1 three-view:
Mike Badrocke

Filmset by SX Composing Ltd

Colour reproduction by Rodney Howe Ltd, Scantrans PTE Ltd, Singapore

Printed in Hong Kong

Introduction

The A-10 is most unusual among modern American combat aircraft. Built in a single model, in strictly limited numbers, for one specialized role, and without a single export order to its name, it is the antithesis of such predecessors as the Phantom or the nearly contemporary F-15 and F-16, which are notable for their popularity and versatility.

Critics would explain the A-10's lack of sales by pointing to its apparently outdated performance figures, its lack of sophisticated avionics and its airliner engines, all of which add up to no more than an absence of spurious glamour. In fact, for its uniquely demanding role of visual-range tank-busting, the A-10 Thunderbolt II– 'Warthog' to its intimates – is uniquely well-suited.

Down on the deck, under the cloud and in visibility that would ground almost any of its contemporaries, it can hide from missile and AA radars for all but the few seconds needed for a devastating gun or Maverick attack; it can out-turn high-speed interceptors; and its gun is as deadly against aircraft as against main battle tanks.

Paradoxically, the Warthog's strengths are a principal reason for the limit on numbers built. Hard to break, easy to mend, with a unique capability to fight, take punishment, regenerate their strength and fight again, A-10s simply do not suffer the kind of attrition associated with other modern fighters.

And other aspects of the design are equally original and impressive. The engines, unique among modern combat aircraft, are ideally suited to the role; the GAU-8/A Avenger cannon gives it a positively awesome punch; and in an era of supersophisticated fighters with appallingly accident-prone systems, an aircraft that has to be flown from the cockpit, rather than by means of a battery of black boxes, is one of the most sought-after assignments the Air Force has to offer.

Development

The requirements of the close air support mission could not be met by the big, complex supersonic jets developed for Tactical Air Command during the 1950s: in Vietnam, they were met instead by slow, propeller-driven aircraft whose virtues were long endurance, good weapon-carrying ability, low-speed manoeuvrability and good visibility. All the latter qualities are embodied in the A-10, which originated in the Attack Experimental programme initiated, at least partly as a result of pressure from the US Army, in 1966, and which has found its main role as a tank-killer on NATO's Central Front.

Close support is one of the least standardized missions in military aviation. It can, perhaps, be best defined as the use of airpower to attack hostile ground forces which are already in contact with friendly troops, or are on the point of engaging them. Some air forces do not even use the term 'close air support' (CAS), preferring phrases that emphasise offensive strike slightly to the rear of the battlefield. The Soviet Union's tacticians believe that the most intimate forms of close support should be the province of the ground forces' own helicopters. The infantry commander cares little for such fine distinctions. He wants some friendly firepower to deal with an imminent unpredicted attack by a superior force, and he wants it without delay.

The Fairchild Republic A-10A, officially named Thunderbolt II and universally known as the Warthog, is the only fixed-wing aircraft in the world which has been designed without compromise for the CAS mission. All of its many unique characteristics stem from CAS requirements, including its low speed, its long endurance, its unparalleled protection and its awesome built-in armament. However, its dedication to the CAS mission has also been the reason why it has been overshadowed by its sinuous supersonic contemporaries.

The basic controversy over CAS is nearly half a century old and still kicking. Is it best handled by a specialized aircraft, or by a fighter with bomb racks?

Advocates of the CAS type argue that the 'fast-mover' fighter can hardly perform the mission at all. Its relative delicacy and poor low-speed handling tend to confine it to a single run against a previously identified or designated target. Their opponents argue that it is foolish to design any aircraft to the requirements of land warfare, to the detriment of its ability to fight and survive in the air.

The Western Allies' experience in the 1939-45 war was decisive. The Luftwaffe's favoured CAS weapon, the Ju 87 dive-bomber, won high renown in the early stages of the war, but the Royal Air Force found its measure and defeated it. The RAF and the US Army Air Force had already ordered quite large numbers of dive-bombers, but hardly any of them were used in action. Instead, the most successful CAS weapons in Northern Europe were Typhoons, Tempests, P-51 Mustangs and P-47 Thunderbolts, second-generation fighters armed with newly developed rocket projectiles and heavy gun armament.

The 1944-45 campaign was to influence planning into the 1960s. Its lessons were fresh in mind when Tactical Air Command was formed in 1947, and when the independent US Air Force followed later that year. One of the first things that the USAF did was to eliminate the 'Attack' category from its designation system, along with the obsolete 'Pursuit'. The fighter-bomber became the backbone of TAC. At the same time, though, the concept of close support began to

melt into the 'strike' mission. TAC's main new project for the 1950s was an aircraft designed to fly at supersonic speed at low level, to navigate to a known ground target in bad weather and hit it with a nuclear bomb: the Republic F-105 Thunderchief.

Fighter design trends

The F-105 typified a great many trends in fighter design. It was bigger and more complex than its predecessors and cost a great deal more to buy and maintain, so there would be fewer of the new aircraft built. Because of its great complexity, it would demand more maintenance, so each aircraft would fly fewer missions and each mission would be preceded by many hours of preparation and equipment checks. The F-105 would operate only from well-equipped bases, safely in the rear of the war zone. Its range was excellent, at a high cruising speed; its endurance, in hours, was poor. In brief, there was no way in which an F-105 unit could respond to a call for immediate support.

By 1960, TAC's less sophisticated fighter-bomber types were getting older. Far from planning a replacement, TAC was busily working on SOR-183, a requirement which defined an aircraft much bigger and more sophisticated than the F-105. Nobody appreciated the implications of this trend more clearly than the customers for close air support in the US Army. For a time, the Army seriously considered acquiring its own

CAS aircraft, and the Northrop N-156F (which had not yet received its first Air Force order) and the Fiat G.91 were both evaluated in 1961. The Army also received presentations on a quaint British machine called the Hawker P.1127. The sight of jet fighters in Army insignia touched off an inter-service dispute over the roles and missions split between the USAF and Army. Finally, the Army had to accept tight restrictions on the types of fixed-wing aircraft which it could operate, but the US Air Force was told by the Defense Secretary, Robert McNamara, to rebuild its ability to provide battlefield air support to the Army.

To begin with, CAS was closely linked to the 'limited war' theories of the time, and to the perceived US need to contain Soviet-inspired 'insurgencies' directed at allied states. The revival of CAS within TAC was originally directed at defeating guerrilla-type forces, using limited effort in an unsophisticated air environment. The first practical application of new 'counter-insurgency' (COIN) air power was to be Vietnam, where the first of the USAF's COIN detachments arrived in late 1961.

COIN operations against concealed ground troops called for the accurate delivery of small weapon loads, and with the weapon-aiming technology of 1961 this meant using an aircraft with good manoeuvrability at low speed. Such a light combat aircraft had been conceived in the late 1950s by North American: a strengthened, re-engined

Left: The A-X specification that gave rise to the A-10 was the product of a long process of analysis of close air support requirements: the resulting prototype is seen here with instrument boom attached to its nose.

Right: Slow, but tough and manoeuvrable at low speeds, and able to loiter for long periods with a heavy weight of ordnance, the A-1E Skyraider proved to be the most useful CAS aircraft available in Vietnam.

adaptation of a surplus T-28A trainer. The French had produced the conversion in quantity, as the Fennec, for use in Algeria, and TAC's Special Air Warfare Center at Eglin AFB, Florida, created the similar T-28D for use by Vietnamese forces and the rapidly growing force of US 'advisors'. A three-service requirement was issued for a successor aircraft: a highly versatile, carrier-capable machine of about the same size, power, warload and speed as the T-28D. This was the Light Armed Reconnaissance Aircraft (LARA), and was to be built in huge numbers for the USAF, Navy and Marines and for US allies.

But plans for LARA were upset by the Viet Cong, who began to demonstrate disturbing proficiency with their Soviet-supplied light anti-aircraft artillery (AAA), mostly of 12.7mm calibre. T-28D losses mounted steadily in 1963-64, and TAC's COIN experts attributed many losses to the type's modest speed. Even before the LARA contest winner – Rockwell's OV-10 Bronco – made its first flight, TAC had decided that it was to be confined to the forward air control mission. By late 1964, there were references to a Super-COIN aircraft with a minimum speed – around 315kt (580km/h).

But the need to replace the increasingly vulnerable T-28D was urgent, and the situation became worse in early 1964 when the heavy-lift contingent of the Vietnam-based attack force – Douglas

B-26s – was grounded en masse by structural problems. Fortunately, a replacement was at hand in the burly shape of the A-1 Skyraider, which had been under evaluation at Eglin AFB since the previous year. The A-1 was not fast, but it was reasonably tough, it was manoeuvrable at low speeds – its massive dive-brakes were an asset – and it had a long

endurance with a heavy weapon load, thanks to the efficiency of its piston engine.

The A-1 proved to be by far the most successful CAS improvisation in Vietnam, and one even shot down a MiG-17 which strayed in front of its four 20mm cannon. It was a decisive participant in many rescue operations, because it

could remain on station and continue to fire long after any jet would have turned for home, out of fuel and ammunition. In the CAS mission, its endurance allowed it to loiter just behind the battle area and respond to a call for support faster than any jet. The A-1's low-speed manoeuvrability, and the all-round visibility from its high-perched bubble canopy (infinitely better than that of any contemporary fighter) meant that its pilot saw targets that a jet pilot would miss, and could keep them in sight as he swung the A-1 around to attack. A small turning radius allowed the A-1 to manoeuvre and turn among hills and low cloud, in conditions where jets were confined to a single pass at the target.

Endurance at a premium

The USAF did use other aircraft for CAS in Vietnam – such as the F-100 and the A-37, a version of the T-37 jet trainer – but none had the A-1's endurance, so they had to be kept on the ground until needed. Too often, they arrived too late, or found the tactical situation had changed, and their pilots could not see targets quickly enough to attack on a single pass. Experience in Vietnam convinced the USAF that a manoeuvrable, long-endurance aircraft, primarily relying on the 'Mark One Eyeball' for target acquisition, was the only way to provide effective CAS. The payload and endurance of the A-1 became the baseline for the Super-COIN studies.

Another piece of the jigsaw dropped into place in 1966, when the USAF ordered the A-7D development of the Navy's Corsair II. This was an aircraft about the same size as the Skyraider, but had a longer range, higher operating speeds and much more sophisticated equipment. Its presence in the TAC inventory would help fight the temptation to upgrade a COIN aircraft into another fast, expensive long-range strike type.

Meanwhile, the increasing strength of the Viet Cong was making the early-

Below left: The A-10's World War II namesake, the P-47 Thunderbolt. Shown here with 2,000lb (907kg) bombs, the P-47 was also a useful tank-buster with guns and rockets.

Below: Another Republic product, the F-105 Thunderchief was designed as a supersonic strike aircraft, but spent much of its career delivering iron bombs over Vietnam.

Bottom: The T-28D attack version of the T-28A trainer, seen here in 1962 at Bien Hoa AB, South Vietnam, with gun pods, rockets and bombs, proved too vulnerable to ground fire.

Below: The USAF's acquisition of the A-7D Corsair II in the late 1960s provided a capable long-range attack bomber and cleared the way for a dedicated COIN aircraft.

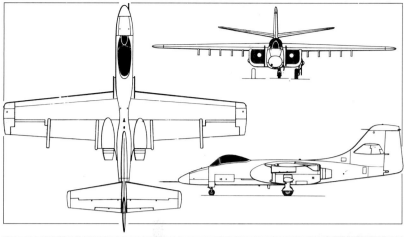

Top: Northrop's A-X contender, the YA-9A, was of conventional layout, with shoulder-mounted wing, single fin, and engines faired neatly into the fuselage sides.

Above: The first YA-9A on an early flight in June 1972. Although the fly-off results were close, the Northrop design lost out in terms of maintainability and survivability.

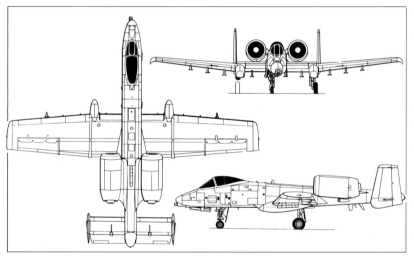

Above left: In complete contrast to the YA-9A, Fairchild's A-10 design was thoroughly unconventional in layout, with low wings, twin fins and podded engines high on the rear fuselage.

Left: The first YA-10A after roll-out from Fairchild's Farmingdale, Long Island, plant. Concern over the company's future, with no major order on its books, was an important factor in the USAF's choice.

Below: Airborne on a test flight, the first YA-10A demonstrates its ordnance-carrying capability.

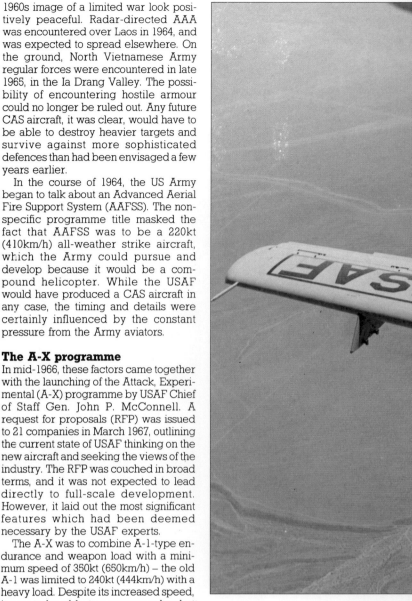

1960s image of a limited war look positively peaceful. Radar-directed AAA was encountered over Laos in 1964, and was expected to spread elsewhere. On the ground, North Vietnamese Army regular forces were encountered in late 1965, in the Ia Drang Valley. The possibility of encountering hostile armour could no longer be ruled out. Any future CAS aircraft, it was clear, would have to be able to destroy heavier targets and survive against more sophisticated defences than had been envisaged a few years earlier.

In the course of 1964, the US Army began to talk about an Advanced Aerial Fire Support System (AAFSS). The non-specific programme title masked the fact that AAFSS was to be a 220kt (410km/h) all-weather strike aircraft, which the Army could pursue and develop because it would be a compound helicopter. While the USAF would have produced a CAS aircraft in any case, the timing and details were certainly influenced by the constant pressure from the Army aviators.

The A-X programme

In mid-1966, these factors came together with the launching of the Attack, Experimental (A-X) programme by USAF Chief of Staff Gen. John P. McConnell. A request for proposals (RFP) was issued to 21 companies in March 1967, outlining the current state of USAF thinking on the new aircraft and seeking the views of the industry. The RFP was couched in broad terms, and it was not expected to lead directly to full-scale development. However, it laid out the most significant features which had been deemed necessary by the USAF experts.

The A-X was to combine A-1-type endurance and weapon load with a minimum speed of 350kt (650km/h) – the old A-1 was limited to 240kt (444km/h) with a heavy load. Despite its increased speed, it was to be able to manoeuvre hard at low airspeeds; the USAF wanted an aircraft which could turn in a limited amount of space, in order to attack an objective without overflying its defences, or make a complete turn in poor visibility without losing sight of the target.

The speed of A-X would not be enough to avoid ground fire completely, so it would be designed to survive when hit. In Vietnam, too many US fighters were being lost to small-calibre or frag-

ment strikes in vulnerable areas, revealing design flaws in most of the service types. Although systems were duplicated, they were seldom protected, and the two channels often ran close together where a single hit would destroy both. In parallel with the A-X programme, several companies were placed under contract to study the specific question of combat aircraft vulnerability.

In addition to its external armament, A-X was to carry a heavy internal gun. Vietnam experience had led the USAF back to the gun as a fighter weapon, and it was the only class of weapon with which a low-cost CAS aircraft could hit a small moving target. A scaled-up version of the very successful General Electric M61 was the obvious starting point. A-X would also have to be cheap, compared with supersonic fighters, and as simple as possible to maintain and operate. It would be designed to use short, unprepared strips, and to function with the limited maintenance facilities available at such bases. The type's low-speed manoeuvrability, and the heavy gun, were intended to eliminate the need for costly automated weapon-aiming systems.

All in all, the A-X requirement was a great deal more difficult than the updated Skyraider which many people thought it was at the time. With the jet engines available at that time, it would not be possible to match the Skyraider's endurance. A low-bypass-ratio engine (such as a Pratt & Whitney TF30 or Rolls-Royce/Allison TF41) has poor propulsive efficiency at low speeds. The A-7, which uses those engines, has excellent range at Mach 0.75-0.8, but will burn fuel almost as fast at half the airspeed. Its loiter capability is therefore limited. Improving propulsive efficiency at lower

Above: Tanker's eye view of a bomb-laden YA-10A during in-flight refuelling trials. The dummy slipway was not connected to the fuel system.

Left: The two YA-10As in formation. Comparative evaluation was carried out at Edwards AFB, California, during the last three months of 1972.

speeds means imparting a lesser acceleration to a larger mass of air, and in 1967 the only established way of doing so was the propeller.

Propellers, however, bring their own problems. Because of the survivability requirements, A-X would have to have two engines, and the speed and short-takeoff-and-landing (Stol) capability desired by the USAF meant that the A-X would have to be quite powerful for its size. The Stol and low-speed manoeuvrability requirements would demand large propellers, so the engines would be well out from the centreline of the aircraft. It became difficult to design the

A-X so that it would be controllable if one engine failed at low speed, just after takeoff. Northrop looked at the possibility of coupling two turboprops in the tail, as on the Learfan business aircraft, but this would have made the entire aircraft vulnerable to a hit on the single propeller and gearbox. An alternative proposal was to install a cross-shaft between the two engines, but this added weight and complexity. The overall effect was that the turboprop-powered A-X became steadily bigger, approaching 60,000lb (27,200kg) maximum takeoff weight, and accordingly more expensive.

While the industry worked on responses to the RFP, the USAF worked on refining the A-X requirement, to minimize the size and cost of the aircraft while ensuring that all the service's essential needs were met, and on setting up the programme structure to avoid the risk of delays and cost escalation. The USAF was in deep political trouble over two major programmes, the F-111 and the C-5, and had no desire to add A-X to the list. Moreover, while cost increases could be tolerated for an advanced-technology aircraft, they would be the end of the road for A-X, which was billed as a low-cost, low-risk concept.

A-X was beginning to gain even greater importance in Air Force planning. Shocked by the lack-lustre performance of its F-4s against obsolescent MiG-17s and boy-racer MiG-21s over Vietnam, and by the sudden advent of the (apparently) awesome Mach 3 Mikoyan Foxbat, the USAF had directed its FX advanced fighter programme towards maximum performance in air-to-air combat. To suggest compromise for CAS or strike was heresy. From 1968-69 onwards, the entire Air Force CAS mission was riding on the A-X; if the A-X did not materialise, the plans for the new fighter would have to be changed, to add some strike capability, and the Army would demand and get all the money it wanted for the AAFSS, which had now

materialised as the ambitious, sophisticated and expensive Lockheed AH-56A Cheyenne.

Four years elapsed between the first A-X discussions and the issue of a final RFP: a long interval, certainly, but understandable in the light of the fact that A-X was a completely new type of aircraft. The most important change during this initial development period came about as a result of improved engine technology. High-bypass-ratio turbofan engines were being run by all the major engine manufacturers, and were proving capable of everything claimed for them. While they had initially been designed for huge freighters and airliners, the technology turned out to be readily 'scaleable'. Small high-BPR engines for a variety of aircraft – airliners as well as military types – were soon under development and seemed to offer modest risks. On the A-X, the high-BPR engines were efficient enough to meet the endurance requirement. They could be mounted close to the centreline, easing the one-engine-out design case, and the adverse stability and trim effects associated with large propellers were absent. The turbofan, with a single fan stage driven directly by a turbine, is also inherently much simpler than the turboprop, with its gearbox and variable-pitch propeller.

Two other changes were related to the adoption of turbofans by nearly all the companies participating in the A-X programme. The speed of the A-X increased toward 400kt (740km/h), closer to the optimum for the turbofan, and the USAF set its final runway-length objective at a somewhat greater value than had been expected earlier: A-X was to operate from a 4,000ft (1,200m) strip at maximum weight. This was a fairly modest aim. With the thrust/weight ratio and the wing loading already dictated by the low-speed manoeuvre requirements, the field-length target could be met without complex high-lift devices or thrust reversal. Again, this helped reduce the weight and cost of the aircraft.

Another significant change of emphasis began to enter the programme in 1967-68. The North Vietnamese Army had, by that time, made their first use of tanks against US forces, and conventional warfare in Europe was once more being considered now that the 'nuclear trip-wire' philosophy had been abandoned. The anti-armour capability of A-X began to be considerably more important. Meanwhile, in June 1967, the Israeli Air Force had succeeded in knocking out a large number of tanks with the 30mm cannon fitted to their Dassault Mystères. What had happened was that while tank guns and frontal armour had made considerable advances since 1945, tanks remained, inevitably, more vulnerable at the rear, on the sides and, particularly, on the top. The 20mm M61 would not suffice though, so the USAF began to draw up requirements for a new gun for A-X, of larger calibre and with a higher muzzle

velocity. This would be a destructive and very accurate weapon, but it would also be a great deal larger than the M61, and it would only fit in a specially designed aircraft. Quietly, and with very little public attention, the A-X turned from a general-purpose bomb truck into a cannon-armed 'tankbuster', a breed which had been considered extinct since 1945.

Specific requirements
The final RFP was issued in May 1970. Performance requirements included a speed of 350-400kt (650-740km/h). The maximum external load was to be 16,000lb (7,250kg), but this could be traded for internal fuel or for 1,350 cannon rounds. The A-X was to be able to carry 9,500lb (4,300kg) of external ordnance and internal ammunition over a 250nm (460km) radius, and loiter for two hours in the target area. Low-speed manoeuvrability was identified as the route to adverse-weather operations. The A-X, according to the USAF, would be so manoeuvrable that it could operate safely and effectively under a ceiling of 1,000ft (305m) with one nm (1.85km) visibility. "Weather conditions worse than this exist only 15 per cent of the

time," noted an official USAF statement, without specifying to what part of the world this figure applied.

Contestants would be assessed on three other requirements. Survivability, or the ability to avoid or survive hits from a range of current and projected Soviet AAA weapons, was the most novel. Fuel system protection, duplicated and dispersed system runs and armour were basic requirements, but the USAF was keen to have an aircraft which could lose large segments of itself and stay airborne.

Simplicity, another prime requirement, was related to survivability in one respect; a survivable aircraft is of little use if it cannot be quickly repaired. But it was also important from the point of view of reducing the unit and operating cost – and saving money for the sophisticated FX. A-X was to use no new or untried technology, both to reduce costs and to eliminate, as far as possible, the danger of problems in the programme. 'Design to cost' was the watchword: if necessary, weight increases would be accepted and performance sacrificed to meet cost targets. Simplicity was also part of the last main requirement, for rapid response. The A-X might be based at

forward operating bases, close to the battle line, for quicker response to any calls for support, and maintenance facilities would be limited.

The programme was novel in another respect; it would be the first in 15 years to involve a head-on, competitive evaluation between two prototypes. This reversion in policy stemmed from the problems with the F-111 programme, which had been launched simultaneously into production and development. Technical problems were encountered, and by the time they were fixed a great many aircraft had been built. It had also been necessary to modify many aircraft on the production line, and costs had escalated enormously.

The revived 'fly-before-buy' philosophy would avoid such problems, because the new aircraft would be flown and thoroughly tested before a production decision was taken. In the case of A-X, which was to be a low-risk design, this aspect of fly-before-buy was perhaps less important than the psychological factor. The manufacturers would be kept under strong competitive pressure until a much later stage in the programme, and by the time they had built and flown prototypes they would have a much greater stake in success.

Six companies responded to the 1970 RFP by the August 10 deadline: Cessna, Fairchild, Boeing-Vertol, Lockheed, General Dynamics and Northrop. The programme was significant, in that the USAF and US Navy had already selected contractors for their other important new aircraft. The A-X was – at that time – the last major combat aircraft programme in sight for many years. The field of contenders was strong. Lockheed and GD were among the most capable of aerospace companies, even if both were in the Pentagon's doghouse over the C-5 and F-111. Cessna had experience with the A-37 Dragonfly. Northrop had shown great expertise in building effective combat aircraft with comparatively low purchase and operating costs. Boeing-Vertol, a helicopter manufacturer, was an unexpected participant, with the only remaining propeller-driven design.

Fairchild – to be more precise, the Republic Aviation Division of Fairchild-Hiller – had learned a great deal from the performance of its F-105 in combat, but had produced no new aircraft since then. Thunderchief production had been terminated prematurely in favour of the F-4C Phantom; Republic had been involved in two separate efforts to develop highly advanced, supersonic, variable-sweep V/Stol fighters, in collaboration with European countries, but neither had borne fruit; and the company had been a finalist in the F-X competition, losing to McDonnell Douglas. Of all the A-X contenders, the Republic organisation was the only one which risked disappearing from the scene as a prime contractor if its bid did not succeed, and its best people were assigned to the preparation of the A-X proposal.

Right: This mock-up of the A-10 forward fuselage was mounted on a rocket-powered sled and used to test the McDonnell Douglas Escapac IE-9 ejection seat at Holloman AFB, New Mexico, in August 1974. Later A-10s were fitted with the Escapac II.

Below: The ejection seat saved the life of this pilot, who banged out after experiencing control problems. One of a batch of six Development, Test and Evaluation machines, the A-10 is carrying Air Force Systems Command markings; the incident occurred during filming of gun firing as part of the successful programme to eradicate the dangerous build-up of explosive gases from the gun barrel experienced with early GAU-8/As.

Weapon for the A-X
Also in 1970, the USAF issued an RFP couched in similar terms for what would now be the primary weapon, the internal gun. Designated GAU-8, it was to be a 30mm weapon with a 4,000 rounds/min rate of fire; the latter requirement effectively dictated that it would be a Gatling-type weapon, with multiple barrels. While the calibre was not as large as that of earlier airborne anti-tank guns, the weapon would make up the lost impact energy in muzzle velocity: 3,500ft/sec (1,067m/sec), equal to the best 20mm weapons in service and considerably better than most heavy cannon. It should be remembered, too, that the size of a

Below: The second YA-10A with its port outer wing and tailfin painted white for spin and recovery testing at **Edwards in November 1974. This aircraft was retired in June 1975 after logging 548.5hr in 354 flights.**

Above: The spin chute container installed on the tail of the second YA-10A, serial 71-1370, to help recovery during spin trials.

gun increases rapidly with greater calibre. The mass of each round rises with the cube of the calibre, and the loads on the breech, the barrel and the feed systems follow suit. Barrel length increases with the calibre and the velocity. By the time the RFPs were issued, it was clear that the GAU-8 would be among the largest guns ever mounted on an aircraft, eclipsing even the 75mm weapons which had been tried in the 1940s. As in the case of A-X itself, the gun was to be selected after a competitive prototype evaluation. Four companies responded to the GAU-8 RFP – General Electric, which had built the original M61, Philco-Ford, Hughes and General American Transportation.

Above: Early firing trials with a prototype of the GAU-8/A 30mm cannon were carried out by the first YA-10A at Edwards AFB from September 1974. The fireballs formed by unburnt gun gas are apparent.

Left: Heavy-duty nose installation used to dispel the gun gases during early GAU-8/A firing trials.

After so many studies of the A-X requirement, the USAF's needs were quite clear, and the final evaluation was quick. Four months after the closing date for proposals, the USAF announced that Northrop and Fairchild would each build two A-X prototypes. Northrop's contract for the YA-9A was worth $28.9 million, and Fairchild would receive $41.2 million for the YA-10A. The main reason for the difference was that Fairchild planned to build an aircraft close to production standards, while Northrop preferred to build something closer to a classic prototype, which would show what the production aircraft could do, but would not necessarily resemble it internally. The decision on the gun was announced later: General Electric and Philco-Ford were to build competing prototypes under $12.1 million contracts. The gun prototypes would thus cost one-third as much as the four A-X contenders themselves. The prototypes would be armed with the trusty M61 while GAU-8 development continued.

A common characteristic of all the USAF competitive flight evaluations or 'fly-offs' in the early 1970s was that the finalists were very different from each

Above: The first DT & E A-10, serial 73-1664, with three fuel tanks and instrumented nose boom during testing at Edwards in mid-1975.

Right: Underside view of the same aircraft carrying 18 1,000lb (907kg) bombs and reflecting the golden rays of the setting sun.

other. This was contrived quite deliberately, because one advantage of the fly-off approach was that a promising, but unconventional configuration or solution could be tested without risking the entire programme if it turned out to have some inherent and unacceptable flaw. The A-X finalists were different in many ways, and gave the USAF a very real choice of design philosophies; the contest was, however, the closest of all the fly-off evaluations.

The differences between the two aircraft started with their external shape. Where the Northrop design followed conventional fighter practice, with a shoulder wing, single fin and engines mounted close to the fuselage, the YA-10A resembled no previous combat aircraft apart from a few last-days-in-the-bunker German projects from 1945. The engines were mounted on the rear fuselage, airliner-style, there were twin fins and rudders and the main landing gear retracted into pods under the wing. The low-slung YA-9A was a design of elegant solidity, with its engines faired smoothly into the fuselage and the fin sweeping upwards from the aft body; its rival was a gangly beast, its long, skinny fuselage and broad wing improbably mated atop a stalky undercarriage.

Another material difference between the two aircraft was the choice of engine. Two high-bypass turbofans in the right thrust bracket were available in the USA. Fairchild selected the General Electric TF34, already under development for the US Navy's Lockheed S-3A anti-submarine warfare aircraft. Northrop chose a smaller engine, the Avco Lycoming ALF 502, which had been launched as a private venture in 1969. It received the military designation YF102-LD-100. It delivered 15 per cent less thrust than the TF34, but was 23 per cent lighter and only just over half as long. It was based on the world's first high-bypass turbofan, the PLF1, which had run in late 1963. The main selling point of the F102 was that it was derived from the T55 turboshaft, which had a long and distinguished record of peacetime and combat service in military helicopters. The YA-9A's cleaner shape largely made up for its lower installed thrust; the mission performance of the two aircraft was very similar, both meeting the

specification, but the YA-10A would do so at slightly higher weights. Both contestants, though, were required to provide performance data with either engine.

Control surfaces
Both A-X contenders featured combined aileron/speedbrake surfaces on their outer wings; these resembled conventional ailerons, but were split into upper and lower panels. When opened, they produced a powerful deceleration effect with virtually no trim change, unlike a fighter-type dorsal or ventral brake. The YA-9A went somewhat further than its rival, featuring a unique side-force control (SFC) system. This linked the speedbrakes and the very large rudder, and could be engaged or disengaged from the cockpit. If the pilot commanded a move to the left, the SFC system would deflect the rudder to the right, opposite

to the usual direction. At the same time, the left speedbrake would open, preventing the aircraft from turning to the right. Instead, the thrust of the rudder would move the aircraft bodily to the left, without turning or banking. With SFC, the pilot could track a ground target without constantly worrying about the bank angle and fuselage direction changes that accompany a conventional turn; Northrop estimated that SFC could double the tracking accuracy of a typical attack.

Before either design left the ground, the entire A-X programme had to survive the first of many critical reviews by Congress. By the end of 1970, there were no fewer than three very active CAS programmes under way in the USA: A-X, the Army's Cheyenne, and the US Marine Corps' acquisition of the Hawker Siddeley Harrier. Congressional critics demanded to know why all three types

were needed. The Department of Defense – which, of course, oversaw all three services – launched its own extensive study of CAS doctrine, tactics and requirements in February 1971. At about the same time, the USAF was working on its own study, TAC 85, which covered the entire spectrum of tactical missions. One of the most significant aspects of these studies was that they marked a break from Vietnam-oriented attitudes, and concentrated instead on the situation in Europe.

Emphasis on Europe
The DoD told Congress that the US military simply did not have anything in service which could perform CAS effectively. Delivery accuracy, acquisition of small tactical targets and response times were all inadequate to a greater or lesser extent. For the first time, the report referred to the imbalance of ground armoured forces in Europe, and to the potency of new and forthcoming Soviet air defence systems (such as the SA-6 missile and the ZSU-23 mobile anti-aircraft gun system, although these were not specifically mentioned in the unclassified version of the report). The DoD argued that the extent of the threat made CAS a critically important mission, and also a very complex one. Each of the three CAS types, in the DoD's view, was best suited to some part of the requirement: "Cheyenne in discrete, responsible, highly mobile units, operating as part of the ground manoeuvre force;

Left: Line-up of early A-10s at Edwards in mid-1975. The two prototypes (furthest from camera) were retired in May and June as soon as three of the six DT & E aircraft (foreground) were available.

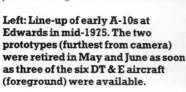

reported on both contestants. The evaluation was planned to include 123hr flying for each type, but eventually the YA-9As flew 146hr in 92 sorties, while the Fairchild aircraft logged 138.5hr in 87 sorties. Just under half the time was spent firing 20,000 rounds from the M61 cannon and releasing 700 'iron' bombs – no guided weapons were used at this stage – while about a third of the flying hours were devoted to performance and handling tests. Flight tests were followed by a week of maintenance demonstrations.

While the fly-off was unquestionably important, it was certainly not the only factor in the evaluation. Systems Command carried out its own theoretical assessment of the competing aircraft in parallel with the fly-off, covering areas which flight-testing could not be expected to explore. These included operational aspects, such as the degree of protection provided against gun and missile attack in the two aircraft; industrial considerations, such as the amount of work needed to set up production, and future concerns, including the potential of each type for development. The two engines were the subject of a parallel evaluation. An unprecedented series of tests was carried out at Systems Command's headquarters at Wright-Patterson AFB, Ohio, where representative components of both A-X designs were set up on stands, blasted with a simulated slipstream from a jet engine, and bombarded with 23mm shells from a Soviet-built anti-aircraft gun, to determine whether their foam-filled fuel tanks would withstand such hits without ignition.

Political pressure

Politically, there was pressure on the Air Force to select Fairchild. The aircraft industry in New York State had historically been dominated by Republic and Grumman. The latter, in 1972, was in serious trouble with the F-14 programme, and there were doubts about its future. Fairchild's Republic division had also been the largest single subcontractor on the Boeing SST programme, scrapped the previous year. Unless Fairchild was awarded the A-X, Long Island's aerospace industry might suffer permanent damage. It was not exactly possible to say the same about Northrop and Los Angeles.

Congressional pressure alone would not be enough to swing an Air Force decision against the service's own assessment, but neither was it in the USAF's interest to let a major contractor lose its capability to design and build a complete military aircraft. Competition was – and remains – a key element in the USAF procurement system, and the service had come to expect at least half-a-dozen responses from qualified suppliers to any of its RFPs. Other things being equal, this factor would tend to favour Fairchild.

Results from the fly-off competition were close. The Northrop type displayed better handling qualities in some respects; the YA-10A proved slightly superior from the maintenance viewpoint; but both aircraft improved on the specification. Systems Command's analysis showed a significant advantage for the Fairchild aircraft in the important area of survivability. The YA-10A, due partly to its unconventional configuration, appeared to be better protected against attack. The most important difference, though, was that the YA-10A was much more representative of a production-type A-X than the YA-9A, something which had been reflected in the higher price quoted and paid for the Fairchild prototypes. This would mean an easier transition to production, with lower risks and smaller learning costs.

Harrier in rapid response to urgent firepower requirements during amphibious operations; and A-X in concentrating heavy firepower, matching selected munitions to different targets, at threatened sectors from dispersed bases". The DoD conceded that the capabilities of the three types might overlap "in less demanding situations", but concluded that all three would be needed for the full spectrum of operations.

The A-X programme survived this first brush with politics, but with some conditions. The A-X would not be launched into full production as soon as a winner emerged from the fly-off. Further testing would have to prove the type's prowess in the CAS role, including its ability to survive against defensive systems and the lethality of its internal gun against armoured vehicles. As the initial development of the GAU-8 was not due to be completed until mid-1973, there

would clearly be some delay to the programme, but the DoD regarded lethality and survivability as essential to the A-X and would not release the type for production until it had proved itself.

The fly-off competition called for both A-X candidates to be delivered by road to Edwards AFB, where they would make their first flights in the hands of company test pilots before being handed over to a specially formed USAF joint test force (JTF). The Air Force evaluation was to start in late October 1972. The YA-10A was the first to fly, taking to the air in the hands of Howard 'Sam' Nelson on May 10, 1972. Its Northrop rival followed 20 days later. The second YA-10A flew on July 21, and the second YA-9A joined the programme on August 23. The manufacturers had five months to unearth and fix any operationally significant problems in the design, because the rules of the

Above: Seen from the cockpit of an A-37, a DT & E A-10 without ordnance but with eight pylons installed, rolls to port over a gun range where M48 and T-62 tanks will be attacked.

contest prohibited any design changes during the JTF evaluation unless safety was in jeopardy. The only externally visible change concerned the YA-10A. Not surprisingly, stalling the aircraft sent turbulent airflow into the TF34s, which responded by stalling themselves. A fixed slot was fitted to the inboard wing to smooth out the airflow. The second YA-10A, too, was involved in the only incident of the test programme, blowing both main tyres in a heavy landing and sustaining minor damage to its nosewheel.

JTF evaluation

These and other problems had all been taken care of by the time the JTF took the four aircraft over, on October 24. The JTF was a new type of organisation, designed specifically to handle the competitive evaluation. It comprised test pilots from USAF Systems Command, which is responsible for the engineering and procurement of all USAF aircraft, and from TAC, which would use the A-X. Other experts were assigned to the JTF from the USAF Logistics Command and the Air Training Command, and their task would be to assess the maintenance requirements of the competing aircraft. All JTF team members worked and

Left: The second DT &E A-10, 73-1665, armed with Hobo and Paveway guided bombs, fires a burst from its cannon during the weapons test programme which it shared with the third pre-production aircraft.

Barely two weeks after the close of the fly-off and maintenance comparison, on January 18, 1973, the USAF announced the selection of the Fairchild aircraft. In the following weeks, the USAF and Fairchild negotiated a $159 million contract, covering ten development, test and evaluation (DT & E) aircraft for further testing. (This batch was later cut to six aircraft by Congress, and the remaining four pre-production aircraft were completed under the first production contract.) The contract included an option for initial production of 48 aircraft, but the A-10 would not be ordered in quantity until further tests of the aircraft had been completed, and the effectiveness of the GAU-8 had been demonstrated.

At the same time, the General Electric TF34 was selected to power the new aircraft. This was not a foregone conclusion, because an Avco-powered A-10 and a GE-powered A-9 had both been studied, and Avco Lycoming was offering a developed version of the F102 with greater power and growth potential. While the F102 was being offered at a considerably lower price than the TF34, the GE engine had one tremendous advantage: it was three years into a full-scale development programme for a military aircraft. The USAF also planned to use eight TF34s to power the Boeing AWACS (the idea was dropped a few weeks later) and large-scale orders held the prospect of lower unit costs in the future. Moreover, Fairchild and GE had worked together on a package of low-risk modifications to the TF34 which would reduce its cost without degrading its performance in the A-X.

Three days before the decision on the airframe and engine was announced, the two GAU-8A prototypes began side-by-side ground firing trials at the Armament Development and Test Center at Eglin AFB, Florida. Initial trials concerned the accuracy and general functioning of the guns; the advanced family of ammunition types was tested from a single-barrel stand in March, and tests proceeded with both guns until a firing rate of 4,000 rounds/min was attained. GE's experience with Gatlings, and the company-funded research on advanced 30mm weapons which it had started in 1968, told heavily in its favour, and it was selected for Phase 2 GAU-8 development in June 1973. GE was awarded a $23.7 million contract for 11 pre-production models, three for quality testing, and eight for installation in the pre-production A-10s.

Unofficial name

A less official event in the history of the programme can also be traced to Eglin AFB and the summer of 1973. Discussing the A-10 in the Tactical Air Warfare Center's *TAWC Review*, Major Michael G. Major closed his article by proposing a name for the new aircraft. Republic's first jet fighter, the F-84, had a less-than-sparkling take-off performance which earned it the nickname 'Groundhog' or just 'Hog'. Its swept-wing development, the F-84F, became the 'Super-Hog', and the concrete-hungry F-105 was christened 'Ultra-Hog'. "What do you suppose the A-10 will be called?" wondered Major. "The 'warthog'?" The name was

Right: Carrying its Paris Air Show number on the engine pod, a 355th TTW A-10 en route back to its base at Davis-Monthan in June 1977.

Above: For trials with Paveway laser-guided bombs and the Pave Penny laser seeker pod, 73-1665 – showing the effects of a strenuous test programme – is equipped with cameras under the nose and tail.

Left: The ability to fly from forward bases close to the battle area was a prime A-X requirement: one of the first production batch of 52 A-10As kicks up the dust as it comes in to land on the dry lake bed at Edwards.

too appropriate not to stick to an ugly beast with a thick hide and dangerous tusks.

The two YA-10As flew from Edwards throughout the rest of 1973 and 1974, although at a slightly lower rate than in 1972. The main thrust of the programme was the definition and completion of the pre-production aircraft, the first of which was due to be delivered at the end of 1974. The No 2 aircraft tested refinements to the design, including a package of aerodynamic changes which reduced drag both in cruising and manoeuvring flight: the wingspan was increased by 30in (76cm), cutting induced drag, the canopy and windscreen shapes were refined, the engine pylons were shortened and streamlined and the landing gear pods were reduced in cross-section. The temporary fixed slats were replaced by automatic retractable slats. All of these were to be incorporated on the pre-production aircraft. The second YA-10A explored the spinning and recovery envelope in late 1974.

Another series of trials took place as a result of Congressional pressure to replace the A-10 with the A-7D. After scaling down the pre-production programme in mid-1973, as mentioned above, the Senate Armed Services Committee threatened to make further cuts and divert the money into additional A-7D orders. In September 1973, it was agreed that the A-10 programme could continue, provided that a second fly-off contest was arranged between a YA-10A and an A-7D. This took place in April-May 1974 at Fort Riley, Kansas. The A-10 was found to offer significant advantages, particularly in less-than-perfect visibility where targets might merge into a dull background. Air Force testimony to Congress after the trials was unanimous: the A-10 was the only aircraft for the short-range CAS mission.

Operationally related testing included the installation of a standard 'slipway' for the USAF flying-boom refuelling system in the nose of the No 1 YA-10. This was a departure from normal fighter practice – most US fighters have receptacles behind the cockpit – but was found to be an improvement. The slipway was not plumbed into the fuel system on the prototypes, which instead took off at high gross weights to simulate the behaviour of the aircraft towards the end of the fuel transfer operation. The refuelling tests were concluded in August; in the same month, a mock-up forward fuselage, attached to a rocket-powered sled, was used for successful tests of the Escapac IE9 ejection seat at Holloman AFB, New Mexico. August 1974 also saw the start of

Above: A formation flight of four early production A-10s assigned to the 355th TTW. The wing's 333rd Tactical Fighter Training Squadron received its first A-10s in March 1976, and was the first operational unit to be equipped with the type, training pilots for service with combat wings.

Left: While two of its aircraft visited the Paris Air Show before going on to tour USAFE bases, three of the 355th TTW's A-10s carried out a series of demonstrations of their capabilities at PACAF bases, including this one in Korea, during June and July, 1977.

Below: A 355th TTW A-10 in the asymmetric colour scheme used for only 17 of the early production aircraft.

a series of unguided launches of the Hughes AGM-65A Maverick television-guided 'fire-and-forget' missile. Along with the GAU-8/A, Maverick was to be a standard weapon for the A-10. Eleven missiles were launched during the first evaluation flights.

Development of the gun and its three types of ammunition – armour-piercing incendiary (API), high-explosive incendiary (HEI) and target practice (TP) – continued in parallel with that of the aircraft. By September 1974, a prototype GAU-8/A was installed in the first YA-10A for preliminary trials. These disclosed a potentially serious problem. The explosive gases generated by the propellant were not being fully burned in the barrel, and the remnants were being expelled and ignited in front of the aircraft, forming a large and dangerous fireball. This was the most serious technical problem facing the A-10 programme towards the end of 1974, but was solved by adding a potassium nitrate additive to the propellant: a technique borrowed from the US Navy's battleship guns. This change also increased the projectile velocity to some degree. The gun itself passed its Critical Design Review in September 1974.

Production problems

Completion of the Critical Design Review on the production-standard airframe, with its aerodynamic changes, provision for the GE gun and other operational equipment, had been announced in May 1974. USAF people at Fairchild's Farmingdale plant, however, were growing concerned about the progress of production. The company had not run a major programme since the F-105 line had closed ten years before; many of its management people lacked experience in production, and the plant's machinery was outdated. (Some of it, one USAF officer asserted, had been used to build P-47s.) Both the cost and schedule targets of the programme were in danger. An Air Force inquiry led to a series of changes in Fairchild production management and organisation, and the USAF increased its staff at

Farmingdale. Fairchild acquired new numerically-controlled machine tools to replace equipment from the F-105 era, and, on the recommendation of the Air Force, placed more of the A-10's critical machined components – the first parts to be assembled in any aircraft, which have the greatest potential to delay or disrupt production – with subcontractors.

Generally, progress with the A-10 was considered to be encouraging by mid-1974, and the GAU-8/A was also going well, although it had yet to be fired from the A-10. The Department of Defense accordingly gave the production programme an amber light at the end of July, releasing $39 million to start production of 52 production A-10As: the 48 aircraft which the USAF had taken on option at the start of the programme, plus the four aircraft which Congress had cut from the original DT & E contract. However, options to buy a smaller quantity were to be kept open. Five months later, with more aircraft and weapon trials completed and the DT & E fleet in final assembly, production of the A-10 was

unconditionally authorized by the DoD.

The first DT & E aircraft was completed at Farmingdale in late 1974, and after preliminary ground tests it was stripped of its wing and empennage and flown to Edwards AFB in a C-5A transport, where it made its first flight on February 15, 1975. (On the previous day, the 1,000th YA-10 flight hour had been recorded.) The first DT & E aircraft was 'heavily instrumented' – that is to say, packed with sensors to measure temperature, vibration and strain in every component, and warrened with wiring runs linking all the gauges to a central digital recording system. It was not fitted with a gun, and its task was to measure and evaluate performance, handling, aerodynamic efficiency, loads and flutter.

The second of the pre-production batch was the first A-10 to make its first

Below: With the wing's old A-7Ds parked in the background, A-10s of the 355th TTW form up on the runway at Davis-Monthan AFB, Arizona.

Left: During 1977 the 354th TFW at Myrtle Beach began to convert to the A-10: here one of the wing's new aircraft refuels from a KC-135.

Below: A pair of 354th TFW A-10s in the new European camouflage scheme in flight with bombs (foreground) and Maverick missiles.

Below: The new standard colour scheme of 30 percent and 50 percent grey was introduced with the 23rd production aircraft.

flight from Farmingdale, on April 26; it was also the first new aircraft to fly from Farmingdale since the last F-105 was completed. Fairchild, however, had sold the company airfield for general-aviation use some years before, and it was too crowded to be used for acceptance-test flying once the production programme got into its stride. By April, it had been decided to move A-10 final assembly and testing to another Fairchild facility at Hagerstown, Maryland, after the completion of the 10th aircraft.

The second DT & E aircraft was to share weapons and systems testing with the third of the batch, which flew on June 10. Both had GAU-8/A cannon installed. From June onwards, one A-10 joined the test programme every month. The fourth DT & E aircraft backed up the first for performance tests, and like the first, it did not have a gun. The fifth would lead

Below: The switch to European camouflage and the Maverick armament carried by this 354th TFW A-10 reflect the type's role.

the initial operational test and evaluation programme, and the sixth would be used for climate testing.

As the second DT & E aircraft joined the test programme in April 1975, the first YA-10A was retired and placed in 'flyable storage' after 467 flights and 590hr. Likewise, the second YA-10A was withdrawn from the programme in June, once the third pre-production aircraft was available. It had flown a total of 548.5hr in 354 flights.

Testing progressed with few problems. By the end of the year, it was revealed that the original weight estimates for the DT & E aircraft – including a 2,000lb (907kg) weight saving compared with the YA-10s – had been optimistic, and that the type was somewhat overweight. The USAF, however, decided that the resulting degradation of overall performance was not critical. One failure occurred during static testing of the fatigue-test airframe at Farmingdale; a minor redesign of a forged fuselage/wing fitting was carried out to solve the problem.

Snags were overshadowed, though, by the performance of the second DT & E aircraft in the first live gun-firing tests, conducted against surplus US M-48 tanks and Soviet T-62s obtained via Israel. The A-10/GAU-8 combination confounded the sceptics, and clearly demonstrated that design aims had been achieved. Accuracy, range and destructive firepower were incomparably superior to anything achieved before. Strikes against the side and top armour of the T-62s, not only with the API ammunition but also with the HEI shells – which had been designed originally for use against softer-skinned vehicles – penetrated the heavy tanks' protection and set off secondary explosions of internal fuel and ammunition. The targets were totally destroyed, by what was effectively point-blank shooting: even at long ranges, the GAU-8/A's velocity was such that ballistic drop and windage could be ignored.

The first production A-10 flew in October 1975, and was delivered to the USAF on November 5. Along with the

next three aircraft off the line – numbers 7 to 10 of the originally planned DT & E batch – it joined the test programme at Edwards AFB, but subsequent aircraft, starting in March 1976, were delivered to the first operational unit. This was the 333rd Tactical Fighter Training Squadron (333 TFTS), which had been designated as the first A-10 squadron in November 1974; part of the 355th Tactical Fighter Training Wing, it was based at Davis-Monthan AFB, Arizona.

Production build-up at Hagerstown was steady, rather than spectacular, and it was April 3, 1978, before the USAF accepted the 100th production A-10A. Present at the handover ceremony were two retired USAF officers: Brig, Gen. Francis S. Gabreski and Col. Robert S. Johnson. Both had distinguished themselves by destroying more than two dozen enemy aircraft in an earlier Republic product, so it was only fitting that the USAF should choose the occasion to give the A-10 a name, one that had been proposed unofficially four years earlier: Thunderbolt II.

Structure

Those who describe the A-10 as the world's ugliest combat aircraft are unjust. The Soviet Mil Mi-24 Hind-D helicopter gunship is the clear winner in this category, by two warts and a proboscis, but the A-10 runs a respectable second. Standing high on its landing gear, its fins and engines reaching out toward the clouds, it is an imposing machine. Its weights and dimensions set it well above most Western support and attack types: it is similar in overall length to the formidable Tornado interdiction-strike aircraft, and its wing span is almost equal to that of the F-111A.

Basic dimensions, though, are misleading; the A-10 may be large, and its maximum take-off weight is considerable, but its normal in-service operating weights are considerably lower. Its configuration springs from the fact that it is designed to excel in a unique flight regime: constant manoeuvre at low speed and low altitudes. Its size is a product of its flight regime and its intended warload.

A heavy weapon load was one of the best features of the A-1, and it was carried over into the A-X requirement. A lesson of Vietnam was that effective intervention in the ground battle called for heavy firepower; dug-in troops or armour were generally unimpressed by the loads delivered by adapted fighters. Endurance requirements also drove the weight upward. The use of external fuel for the normal mission was ruled out from the survivability standpoint, and this meant all the fuel had to be accommodated internally. Morover, the need to protect the internal fuel compromised the conventional fighter-design approach, which is to use every available cubic inch in the air-frame for fuel.

The need for long endurance, and the low operating speeds, ruled out that great weight-saver, the afterburner. The result was higher engine weight for a given thrust level. The advent of the high-BPR turbofan was a major breakthrough, because its low fuel consumption helped make up for that weight penalty.

A-X also set standards for protection around vital areas – the pilot, the fuel system, and the internal ammunition – so that part of the empty weight was virtually independent of the overall size of the aircraft. Given a certain 'defeat level' – the maximum strike which the aircraft must survive – the amount of armour around the cockpit, for example, was the same however large or small the aircraft might be.

These requirements in themselves would have driven A-X beyond the size

Below: Although of unconventional layout, the A-10 prototype, seen here during final assembly, was built using conventional materials and straightforward techniques.

and weight of the Skyraider. As the requirement evolved toward tank-busting, however, the weight of a phenomenally large cannon installation, several times as heavy as an M61, had to be figured into the equation. So did the added airframe size, weight and drag incurred by carrying such a weapon internally, together with the large quantity of ammunition needed for even tens of seconds of firing time. While the A-10 may look large and beefy, its armour, its gun and its ammunition amount to some 25 per cent of its empty weight. It is no larger than an effective platform for the GAU-8/A, armoured to the levels specified by A-X, needs to be.

Wing design

Given the size and weight of an aeroplane, the next feature to be defined is the wing. In the case of the A-10, as with most combat aircraft, the main factors behind the wing design are speed and manoeuvre; other factors, such as range and field performance, tend to fall into place.

The high end of the speed envelope in

Above: The size and weight of the A-10 were largely dictated by the requirement for the massive cannon installation, and the need for sufficient protection to enable it to survive close-quarter tank-busting.

the A-X requirement was not demanding. The maximum operating speed was to be only 400kt (740km/h), and the Fairchild designers selected a maximum design speed (VD) of 450kt (833km/h), allowing a normal safety margin in case a pilot allowed his aircraft to overspeed in combat. Wing designers care more about Mach number, or the relation of speed to the speed of sound, than pure airspeed; in the case of the A-10, the maximum speeds are to be attained at sea level, where the local speed of sound is higher than at medium altitude, so the wing does not have to be designed for more than Mach 0.68. It is possible to encounter high-Mach buffet at such speeds, particularly if the aircraft has to manoeuvre, but the A-10 is not required to manoeuvre tightly at its top speeds.

USAF tactics of the late 1960s were another important factor in the wing design. Attack aircraft, including the A-X, were not generally required to fly for long periods at high speed and low level. 'Ingress' profiles were invariably flown more than 1,000ft (305m) above ground level, in level flight above the roughest air. This, combined with the modest speed, meant that there was no need for the A-10 to have the short, swept, highly loaded wing that were required by contemporary Royal Air Force tactics, for example.

The peak performance of the A-X specification, instead, called for the ability to turn in a small radius and short elapsed time, at modest airspeeds; the A-10, pulling a 3.25g turn at 275kt (510km/h), can manoeuvre in a smaller radius than a fast-jet fighter, and can actually change heading more quickly. The implications of low speed and high g are important. The total drag generated by any aircraft is made up of a number of components, most of which increase with the square of the airspeed. A major exception is induced drag, or the drag due to lift, which increases with the lifting force generated by the wing. In a 3g turn at 275kt, the lift and the induced drag are at three times their normal value, but the other components of airframe drag are still modest. The main thrust of the A-X aerodynamic design, therefore, was to cut down the induced drag in a medium-speed manoeuvre, and the best way to do this was to increase the wingspan.

The A-10 design benefited from the steady advance in the basic design of wing sections. Classic wing sections of

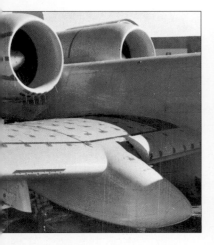

Above: Tufts attached to a YA-10's wings to monitor the airflow, and the stall slats fitted to smooth turbulence at high angles of attack.

Right: Assembly of the A-10 port, starboard and centre wing sections prior to mating with the fuselage.

the 1950s produced most of their lift close to the leading edge; this was to say that the airflow over the wing underwent a single rapid acceleration at this point. This made the wing prone to buffet at even modest Mach numbers, and the only way to delay the buffeting was through the use of sweepback or a thinner section. Thin-section wings are heavier for a given strength, because the spars are not as deep (think of the way beams are placed in a building) and are less efficient at low speeds. In the 1960s, though, the use of computers enabled aerodynamicists to improve their mathematical 'models' of the airflow over the wing. This allowed them to design new

sections in which the lift was more evenly distributed along the chord; they were called 'rooftop' sections, because a chart showing chordwise lift distribution was more symmetrical, like a house roof. Rooftop-section wings could be deeper, and hence lighter, for an equivalent Mach number.

The A-10 accordingly has a long-span, lightly loaded wing, which allows excellent low- to medium-speed turning performance with low drag and a low power requirement. The wing has a rooftop section and a 16 per cent thickness/chord ratio. The deep section makes it possible to build a wing which is reasonably light, has a long span and a high

aspect ratio, and can withstand high g loadings. The depth of the wing, and its bluff leading edge, make for high lift and efficiency at low speeds. Another drag reduction is provided by the down-turned Hoerner wingtips, which act as small, lightweight endplates, reduce vortex flow at the tips and improve aileron effectiveness near the stall.

The big, thick wing also provides ample lift for take-off and landing, meeting all the A-X field-length requirements without the use of complex high-lift devices. The A-10 has classic area-increasing Fowler flaps, driven out along curved tracks to increase the area and camber of the wing. Fairchild did study

alternative wing designs, with less area and double- or triple-slotted flaps, but the increased complexity and cost more than cancelled out the reduction in weight, while straight-line drag and manoeuvrability would have been somewhat worse. The simple Fowler flaps create little additional drag when extended, and can be partially lowered for manoeuvre at very low speeds.

Another advantage of the generously sized wing is that the flaps need extend over only part of the span, leaving room on the trailing edge for large ailerons for effective low-speed roll control; the A-10 has no wing spoilers. The ailerons also incorporate the only unconventional feature of the mainly straightforward aerodynamic control system. Each aileron is split on the horizontal plane, aft of its leading edge. An actuator and linkage in the aileron leading edge drive the two sections apart to form a powerful airbrake. This arrangement gives effective deceleration with virtually no trim change, unlike a dorsal or ventral brake, and does not interfere aerodynamically with the empennage as fuselage-side brakes can do. Similar airbrakes were used on the Northrop YA-9A; in fact, the devices were originally invented by Northrop in the 1940s for its flying-wing designs.

Low-wing advantages

While most contemporary attack aircraft, including the Northrop YA-9A, had shoulder-mounted wings, Fairchild chose a low-wing configuration for the A-10, for a number of reasons. The most important was that the A-X requirement called for at least ten separate weapons pylons under the aircraft. With a low wing it is possible to put the most highly loaded pylons under the fuselage itself, and, generally, to concentrate the heaviest stores near the centreline. This substantially reduces the rolling inertia of the aircraft with a maximum weapon load, and improves its handling. The low wing also provides for a wide-track landing gear with a simple retraction sequence. Some aspects of ground handling are simplified; it is easier to work around the aircraft with the engines running, for instance. On the debit side, all the maintenance has to be done with ladders and platforms.

The wing design is the key to the A-10's performance in the most important flight regime, sustained low- to medium-speed manoeuvre. This regime dictates the installed thrust, so there is plenty of excess thrust available to meet the comparatively relaxed straight-line speed requirement. Reducing drag by the classic means – streamlining, blending and fairing, and reducing surface area - was not necessary to meet the specification and was therefore not considered worthwhile. It can also be argued that achieving, say, a five per cent reduction in clean airframe drag is a futile exercise

Above: The A-10 fuselage assembly line. Long and deep, the fuselage accommodates the pilot and gun, forward, the fuel tanks amidships, and the engines aft.

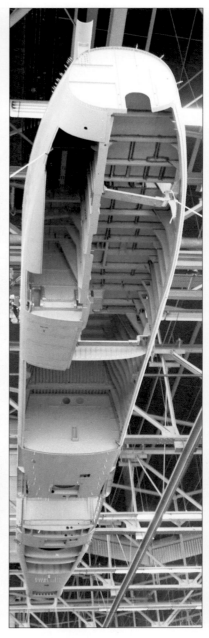

Above: The fuselage shell, showing the massive gun compartment and smaller nosewheel well, with the pilot's armoured 'bathtub' above, is hoisted along the line.

Above: One stage further along, the fuselage, with nose cone in place, gun installed and nose gear hydraulics fitted, is moved into position for mating with the wing assembly.

Above: The imposing, long-legged aspect of the A-10 on the ground is a result of the low-mounted wing and wide-track landing gear.

Right: The second DT & E A-10 with avionics and armament bay doors open for final installation of equipment prior to roll-out.

on an aircraft which will spend most of its life carrying a very large, drag-evoking external payload. Recognizing these factors, Fairchild designed the A-10 fuselage, engine location and empennage according to the demands of utility as well as those of aerodynamics.

The first requirement in the fuselage design is capacity. In most aircraft, a big, thick wing provides the natural home for the fuel, but it was clear from the start of the A-X programme that large wing tanks presented an unacceptably large vulnerable area to the enemy. Instead, the A-10 carries most of its fuel in fuselage tanks, which have a much higher ratio of volume to surface area. To minimize changes in trim as the fuel was used, the tanks were located in the centre fuselage, above the wing.

The forward fuselage is designed around the GAU-8/A cannon and its ammunition drum. The weight of the latter can drop by more than 1,000lb (454kg) as propellant and projectiles are expended (the cartridge cases are recycled back into the drum) so it is located to the rear of the gun, just ahead of the fuel tanks and close to the centre of gravity. The sheer power of the gun itself defines its position. The mass of its shells, its muzzle velocity and its rate of fire generate a constant recoil thrust of 9,000lb (40kN). Unless the recoil thrust vector was aligned precisely on the aircraft's centreline, this would make accurate shooting impossible.

Blast from the gun means that the muzzle must be well clear of any structure, so the only possible location is the nose of the aircraft, right on the centreline. The gun is set below the centre of gravity, so the firing angle is very slightly depressed (by about 2deg) to eliminate any pitch change. The YA-10As featured an automatic elevator compensator, to counter any pitch effects from firing the gun, but this was found to be unnecessary. The seven-barrel rotary gun is offset slightly to the left, and its mechanism is arranged so that the firing barrel is in the nine o'clock position, placing it exactly on the centreline. This makes room for the nose landing gear, which retracts into the right side of the fuselage.

The A-10's long forward fuselage provides room for the 21ft (6.4m) weapon, and the pilot occupies a lofty perch above the feed and breech mechanism. The narrow, flat-sided fuselage, the short nose and the bubble canopy, set well above the wing plane, give the A-10 pilot an all-round view matched by few other aircraft. The forward fuselage design also provides ample room for a second cockpit, which can be accommodated by rearranging some of the internal avionics. (Otherwise, the only change in the design of the two-seater is a slight increase in the size of the tailfins, to compensate for the added side area.)

The rear fuselage is the controversial part of the A-10 design, aesthetically and functionally. The skinny tail section carries the two engines, mounted high on the rear fuselage in airliner style, and the twin-fin tail assembly. It looked strange in the extreme to anyone used to fighter design, but Fairchild had sound reasons in its favour.

The only basic requirement affecting the location of the A-X's engines was that they should be far enough apart that a single hit would not disable both. To Fairchild's designers, it seemed that a conventional installation, with the engines under the wings, eliminated too much of the stores-carrying space on the

Left: The finished product, its bluff lines betraying few concessions to aesthetic considerations, but with an air of purpose and aggression in its strictly functional design.

aircraft. This was particularly true with the fat high-bypass engines, which were being used for the first time on a combat type. Neither were these engines very suited to being built into the fuselage, because of their large airflow requirements and their bulk. It seemed less risky, aerodynamically speaking, to house the engines in straightforward pods with short inlets. Fairchild studied overwing pods, as used on the unsuccessful German VFW 614 jet feederliner, but it would have proved difficult to change the engines without using special lifting equipment, particularly in the confines of a standard concrete hangarette.

The high-mounted rear-fuselage location which was finally chosen has a number of advantages. The engines are well out of the way of any dirt or foreign objects thrown up from the nosewheel when operating from unimproved strips; this is important, because high-bypass engines make superb vacuum-cleaners when placed too close to the ground and their high-pressure cores are very sensitive to erosion caused by dirt and grit. The inlets are also well to the rear, allowing gun gases more time to disperse. Also, as noted earlier, the engines can be kept running while the aircraft is being served and re-armed. One drawback of this arrangement, the fact that changes in thrust could change the trim of the aircraft in pitch, has been avoided by canting the engine nozzles 9deg upwards relative to the rest of the engine.

Tail layout

Rear-engined airliners have mid-set or high tail units, but the risk of a 'deep stall' – a condition in which the wing is stalled, the aircraft is sinking, and the tailplane, trapped in the turbulent wake of the wing and engine pods, has no power to recover the aircraft – immediately ruled out such a layout for the A-10, so the tail is low. Twin fins are partly a result of the engine location. It was felt that the engines could create some odd airflows around the rear fuselage, and might cause spin-recovery problems by shedding turbulent wakes on to a conventional single fin. The complexity of a twin-fin layout is justified, because it is almost impossible for both fins to be rendered ineffective at the same time.

Where the resulting layout scored very high points was in survivability. Control power in pitch and yaw can be retained even if one side of the entire empennage is shot away. More important, though, is the protection afforded to the engines. The fuselage and wing tend to conceal one or both of the engines from groundfire, from many different angles. The vertical and horizontal tail surfaces form what is almost a shroud around the engine exhausts, helping protect the aircraft against early-technology infra-red homing missiles: these weapons, such as the SA-7 Strela, need to 'see' the hot metal of the jetpipe before they will lock on to a target.

Testing of the YA-10s revealed some not unexpected problems with the engine installation. When the wing stalled, turbulent airflow from the wing-fuselage junction entered the inlets and stalled the compressors. The solution was to fit a flow-smoothing slat to the wing, inboard of the landing gear pods, which extended automatically under hydraulic power when the angle of attack exceeded the stall angle. A stall strip – a small spanwise fence, a few inches long

Right: The capacious forward fuselage proved readily capable of accommodating a second cockpit, and the first DT & E A-10 was converted to two-seat configuration for evaluation purposes.

Fairchild A-10A Thunderbolt II cutaway

1 Cannon muzzles
2 Forward radar warning antenna (one each side)
3 ILS antenna
4 Air refuelling ramp door
5 Air refuelling receptacle
6 AAS-38 Pave Penny laser seeker pod
7 Rudder pedals
8 Hinged windscreen panel (for instrument access)
9 Head-up display
10 Control column
11 Pilot's instrument display
12 Engine throttle levers
13 McDonnell Douglas ACES II ejection seat
14 Canopy jettison strut
15 Canopy actuator
16 Leading edge stall strip
17 Starboard wing stores pylons
18 Cockpit canopy cover
19 Pitot tube
20 Starboard navigation and strobe lights
21 Starboard aileron
22 Split aileron/airbrake
23 Airbrake operating jack
24 Aileron hydraulic actuator
25 Aileron tab
26 Cockpit air valves
27 IFF antenna
28 Tab balance weight
29 Anti-collision light
30 UHF/Tacan antenna
31 Starboard single slotted Fowler flaps
32 Flap guide rail
33 Flap hydraulic actuator
34 Fuselage fuel cells
35 Conditioned air delivery duct
36 General Electric TF34-GE-100 turbofan engine
37 Engine oil tank
38 Engine accessory equipment gearbox
39 Bleed air ducting
40 Air conditioning system intake and exhaust duct
41 Heat exchanger
42 Fire extinguisher bottle
43 Starboard tailfin
44 X-band antenna
45 Rudder mass balance
46 Rudder
47 Fan air exhaust duct
48 Core engine exhaust duct
49 Trim tab actuator
50 Elevator tab
51 Starboard elevator
52 Elevator hydraulic activators
53 Rear radar warning receiver
54 Tail navigation light
55 Port elevator
56 Port tailfin
57 Rudder hydraulic actuator
58 Formation light
59 IFF antenna
60 Elevator mechanical linkage
61 UHF/Tacan antenna
62 VHF/AM antenna
63 Fuel jettison
64 Air system ground connection
65 Hydraulic reservoir
66 VHF antenna
67 Hydraulic system ground connectors

68 APU exhaust
69 Auxiliary power unit (APU)
70 Air conditioning unit
71 Port Fowler flaps
72 Flap self-aligning torque shaft
73 Trim tab control rod
74 Aileron trim tab
75 Split aileron/airbrake
76 Strobe light
77 Port navigation light
78 Port aileron
79 Cambered wing tip fairing
80 Airbrake operating jack
81 Aileron hydraulic actuator
82 ECM pod
83 Aileron mechanical linkage
84 Flap hydraulic actuators
85 Hydraulic retraction jack
86 Main undercarriage pivot bearing
87 Chaff/flare dispenser
88 Forward-retracting mainwheel
89 Leading edge stall strip
90 Port wing stores pylons
91 Maverick air-to-ground missile
92 Wing centre section integral fuel tank
93 Main undercarriage wheel housing
94 Inboard wing stores pylon
95 Pressure refuelling connection
96 Slat hydraulic actuators
97 Inboard leading edge slat
98 Fuselage stores pylons (3)
99 Multiple ejector rack
100 Rockeye cluster bomb
101 Airflow smoothing strakes

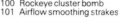
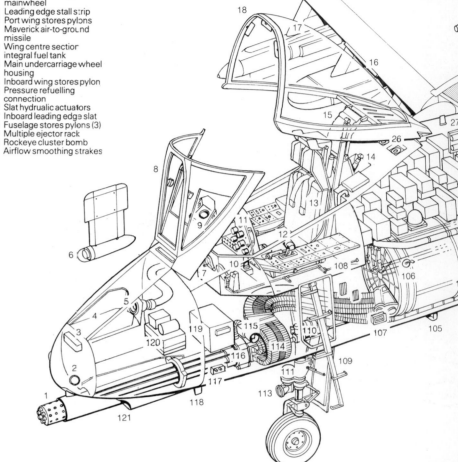

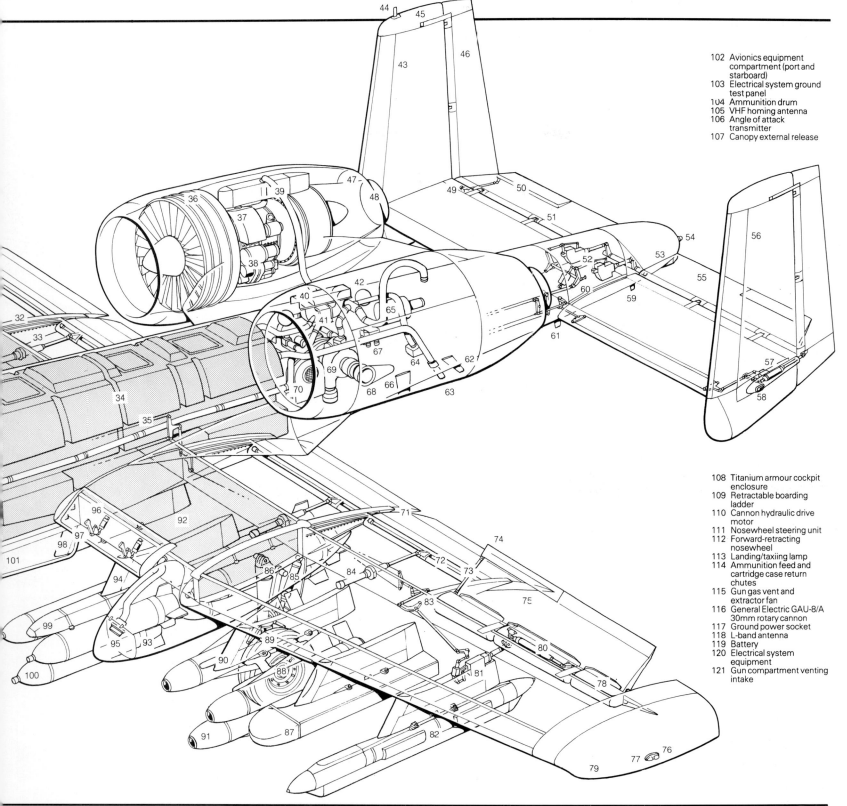

102 Avionics equipment compartment (port and starboard)
103 Electrical system ground test panel
104 Ammunition drum
105 VHF homing antenna
106 Angle of attack transmitter
107 Canopy external release

108 Titanium armour cockpit enclosure
109 Retractable boarding ladder
110 Cannon hydraulic drive motor
111 Nosewheel steering unit
112 Forward-retracting nosewheel
113 Landing/taxiing lamp
114 Ammunition feed and cartridge case return chutes
115 Gun gas vent and extractor fan
116 General Electric GAU-8/A 30mm rotary cannon
117 Ground power socket
118 L-band antenna
119 Battery
120 Electrical system equipment
121 Gun compartment venting intake

Above: The short nose and high-mounted cockpit with bubble canopy give the A-10 pilot a superb view, readily apparent in this photograph of an 18th TFS pilot preparing for a mission from Eielson AFB, Alaska.

– was attached to the outboard leading edge to restore the natural stall warning. Two other devices were also added to cure the wing-engine interaction: prominent vertical strakes, fitted to the fuselage beneath the leading-edge wing root, and a trailing-edge fillet. Otherwise, the A-10 is aerodynamically straightforward, devoid of ventral fins, strakes, vortex generators and other fixes.

The final element in the A-10's unusual shape is provided by the main landing gear, which retracts forward into prominent underwing pods. This arrangement has a number of advantages, and the extra drag which it creates is not critical to the A-10. Unlike a sideways-retracting gear, it takes up little stores-carrying space beneath the wing. (The A-1 had a rearwards-retracting gear, for the same reason.) The entire landing-gear mechanism is attached beneath the wing itself, and the wheel is stowed ahead of the front spar, so there are no cut-outs in the structure.

The retraction mechanism is simple, and all three of the undercarriage legs retract forward; this is the ideal arrangement if the hydraulics are gone and the

Above: The A-10's forward-retracting landing gear legs, simple and rigid, with single wheels and low-pressure tyres, were designed to lower under gravity and wind resistance in the event of hydraulics failure, and the main gear and wheels are stowed in pods to maximize stores loading.

Right: Even in the event of landing gear collapse, the configuration should ensure that the main airframe structure sustains minimum damage.

gear must free-fall into the locked position, because gravity and the airstream both help to extend the gear. If even this next-to-last resort fails, the A-10 gear is designed, like those of the DC-3 or B-17, so that the mainwheels protrude from the gear pods and are free to rotate in a belly-landing. The A-10, in theory, will come to rest on its mainwheels and the lower tips of the fins with barely a bent antenna.

The landing gear itself is simple. The A-10 is designed to use short strips of prepared concrete, of the type that would be left on an airfield where the main runway had been cut in two by bombs, but is not really a rough-field aircraft. The landing gear, therefore, has simple rigid legs rather than more complex levered-suspension units, and there is only one wheel to each leg, carrying a single low-pressure tyre.

Odd as the A-10 may appear, its design has avoided any trace of unusual or unexpected handling qualities. This was a fundamental A-X requirement, and was one of the most important factors in the original fly-off competition; the USAF's view as that the A-X pilot, flying, navigating and acquiring targets at low level with a minimum of artificial help, would have no time to deal with any idiosyncratic handling behaviour.

A-10 pilots report that the aircraft feels much smaller than it looks, to the point where it is necessary to bear in mind that

Left: Preparing for takeoff during Operation Gunsmoke '81 at Nellis AFB, A-10 pilots enjoy an unmatched all-round view from their cockpits, while only minimal ground support equipment clutters the flight line.

the wingtip may be nearly 30ft (9.15m) closer to the ground than the pilot in a steep turn over rolling terrain. The aircraft will tolerate a great deal of abuse, and gives plenty of notice when the limits of its tolerance are approached. The A-10 will remain controllable after the stall, and will only spin if pro-spin controls – full nose-up pitch and full rudder – are applied and held for several seconds; it will recover as soon as the controls are released.

Overall, the aircraft has been summed up as "an easy aircraft to fly safely, but difficult to fly precisely". Perhaps the

A-10 production manufacturing plan

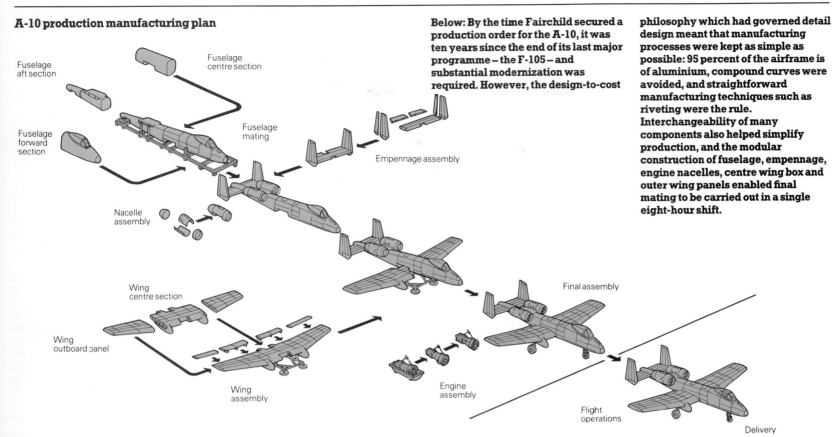

Fuselage aft section

Fuselage forward section

Fuselage centre section

Nacelle assembly

Fuselage mating

Empennage assembly

Wing centre section

Wing outboard panel

Wing assembly

Engine assembly

Final assembly

Flight operations

Delivery

Below: By the time Fairchild secured a production order for the A-10, it was ten years since the end of its last major programme – the F-105 – and substantial modernization was required. However, the design-to-cost philosophy which had governed detail design meant that manufacturing processes were kept as simple as possible: 95 percent of the airframe is of aluminium, compound curves were avoided, and straightforward manufacturing techniques such as riveting were the rule. Interchangeability of many components also helped simplify production, and the modular construction of fuselage, empennage, engine nacelles, centre wing box and outer wing panels enabled final mating to be carried out in a single eight-hour shift.

Left: From the 11th aircraft onward, final assembly of A-10s was transferred to Fairchild's facility at Hagerstown, Maryland, where the company was able to conduct flight testing, its old airfield at Farmingdale having become too cluttered to permit such activity. Here one of the first production batches reaches the end of the assembly line, where the engines are installed and final checks are carried out on the structure and systems, though the line has been cleared for the photographer.

strongest testimony to the A-10's basic flying qualities is that Fairchild selected a very similar configuration when it competed for the USAF's Next Generation Trainer (NGT), and won the contest with what became the ill-fated T-46A.

Internal arrangement

Beneath the skin, the design of the A-10 reflects two main considerations: survivability and design-to-cost. The ability to take hits from a variety of weapons, and survive, pervades both the structure and the systems of the A-10; design-to-cost mainly affects the construction and manufacture of the aircraft.

Design-to-cost was a new philosophy for military aircraft, but has always been a way of life for the designers of light aircraft and, to a limited extent, the airliner industry. While military aircraft, even the most exotic types, were never

designed and built with total disregard for cost, the importance of price decreased rapidly with the move from basic to detailed design. The manufacturing cost would be estimated before any of the detail drawings were prepared, on the basis of the manufacturer's experience with earlier aircraft and the relative complexity of the new aircraft's structure and systems. The customer would base his procurement plan on that estimate.

Once detail design started, however, performance took priority over cost. If a part proved more highly loaded than had been expected, the normal practice was to make it from a higher-grade material and to accept the resulting cost increase. The same would be true if an assembly procedure was more complex than expected. On the other hand, there was no strong incentive to look for ways

in which components could be made more simply, or manufactured from cheaper material than had been envisaged. It was therefore inevitable that costs would increase during the design and development stage.

Under the design-to-cost approach, the manufacturing cost was to be estimated, as usual, as part of the basic design: the A-X requirement set a $1.5 million cost target for the entire aircraft. What was new was that the cost was to be held down to the design level, even if it meant increasing weight and degrading performance. This policy was easier to implement on the A-10 than on a high-performance fighter, because a given mass of excess weight at 3g saps only one-third as much performance as the same mass at 9g. Nevertheless, the cost target was not easy to reach, and fundamentally affected the design.

Cost considerations

Design-to-cost, to begin with, ruled out the use of promising advanced composite materials. Closely contemporary designs such as the F-15 and F-16 used such materials to save weight, but, at the time, the costs of mass-producing composite components could not be safely predicted. A-X would be a conventional light-alloy aircraft, with the exception of some specialized components. The well-proven 7075 and 2024 alloys were chosen, due to their known resistance to stress and chemical corrosion.

During development, any proposed weight-saving was examined for its effect on manufacturing costs. A yardstick of $75/lb ($165/kg) empty weight was used, and if a proposed change cost more per unit saved, it was automatically discarded. Conversely, if a design change would add weight, but save more than $75/lb of extra weight, it would stand a chance of being implemented. This was the first time in a military aircraft programme that an actual dollar value had been put on empty weight.

Another basic principle, followed throughout the design and apparent in the external shape of the A-10, was the avoidance of 'double curvature': as far as possible, the A-10's shape is composed of flat planes or cylindrical or conical sections, reducing the need for slow and costly stretch-forming processes in the manufacturing stage. The fuselage sides are flat; the engine nacelles are cylindrical, rather than teardrop-shaped. Fuselage panels are overlapped and riveted, avoiding the smoother but more complex butt-jointing.

The A-10 is also unique in the degree to which components are interchangeable between the left and right sides of the aircraft: the fins and rudders, main landing gear, wing-root slats, inboard flaps, many fuselage skin panels and all pylons are examples. It was the first twin-jet USAF aircraft on which the engines were not 'handed', and this has now become a requirement for other new USAF types.

The advantages of this philosophy are two-fold: it cuts production cost, by doubling the output of a single part, and it simplifies spares support. In wartime, it may be critical, because the only spares that are any use at all are those that can be found on the base, whether in the normal supply system or aboard a damaged or otherwise inactive aircraft.

A related thrust in the production engineering of the A-10 was to ensure that components would be interchangeable between individual aircraft. This is not always the case: some aircraft have major components which are individually fitted at the factory, and a piece from another aircraft or an 'out of the crate' spare may fit only after precise, time-consuming adjustments, if at all.

Ultimately, the A-10 taught the USAF a lesson in manufacturing economics. After all the effort put into reducing the designed-in cost of the airframe, the Department of Defense revised its budget plans and authorised initial production of only 15 A-10s a month, rather than the 20 aircraft originally planned. This raised the price of the aircraft from the target of $1.5 million to $1.8 million. The USAF itself requested some changes in the avionics fitted to the aircraft, further increasing the price to $2 million. (These figures are compared to the target price and expressed in the same 1970 values; the dollar cost of A-10s as finally delivered was, of course, much higher due to general economic inflation.) Against this 33 per cent increase in the basic cost of the aircraft, the cost savings made through detail design seemed rather insignificant.

Survivability

The other major influence on the internal design, survivability, was equally new as a philosophy. It is strange but true that, before 1968, the ability of an aircraft to absorb battle damage and survive – specifically, to regain its base, with its pilot unharmed, and be repaired to fight again – had never been systematically studied. It was known that some aircraft were good in this respect (such as the B-17) and some were bad (the B-24), but there was no telling, or even guessing, which was the better aircraft until they were committed to combat.

Part of the reason for this state of affairs was a lack of basic data. Vietnam changed the situation. A great many modern aircraft, of a great many types, were used. The defensive fire was more intense, and more dangerous, than anything encountered since 1944-45, and came from a wide range of contemporary weapons. Modern ejection seats were more reliable under a wider range of circumstances; pilots were more easily tempted to stay with a damaged aircraft, if only to increase their chances of rescue by friendly units, and came back to report how they had been shot down.

F-105 experience

Survivability data began to arrive in quantity: the picture was mixed and confusing. One F-105 survived a direct hit on the wing from a 85mm AAA shell, and another was perforated in 87 places by an SA-2 missile and regained its base. But other F-105s were felled in seconds by small-calibre or fragment strikes. The same paradoxical situation applied to other types; Fairchild, however, had an early start in the field, because its F-105 bore the brunt of the Rolling Thunder operations in 1965-68, and F-105 experience was the first large single body of data. Before the A-X programme was initiated, too, Fairchild was upgrading and hardening the surviving F-105s.

It was soon found that the inconsistency of the hit-survival record stemmed directly from the fact that the question had never been seriously investigated. Structural design was driven by strength requirements, and systems design by reliability. While the F-105, designed for supersonic low-level flight, was structurally tough, and would stay together at reduced airspeeds after suffering quite serious damage, the designers had seen no reason not to run the two independent hydraulic systems close together in the belly of the aircraft. A minor strike in this area could knock out the F-105's hydraulics and, in consequence, its flying controls.

The positive lesson drawn from this experience was that survivability could be dramatically increased by attention to a few key areas, and by improvements which added only a modest amount to the empty weight; there was no need to encase the entire aircraft in an armoured carapace.

Guns were the main cause of losses in Vietnam, particularly in the close support mission. Often, the main function of

the SA-2 missile was to force the attackers to use low altitude, within the range of AAA. Cannon projectiles were taken as the measure of the A-10's survivability. Among the most dangerous of these was the 23mm armour-piercing incendiary shell, lethal against fuel tanks; direct hits from 57mm guns were also encountered, but these, like SAMs, were more dangerous as fragments. Since then, the defensive armoury has been modernized; however, studies of vulnerability have shown that the effectiveness of protection does not decline abruptly as the calibre of the threat increases.

Another batch of combat data concerned the vulnerability of the aircraft to damage in different areas. No fewer than 62 per cent of losses of single-engined aircraft, in Vietnam and the Middle East, were caused by damage to the fuel system; 18 per cent to pilot incapacitation; 10 per cent to flying-control damage; 7 per cent to loss of engine power; and 3 per cent to structural damage. These losses reflected heavy missile kills as well as gunfire; however, the A-X operational envelope would be biased towards heights and speeds where AAA would be more effective. The A-X also embodied a new vulnerable zone, in the shape of a very large drum of ammunition. The loss statistics were an indication of what to do on A-X, but not a complete guide.

Survivability has been taken into

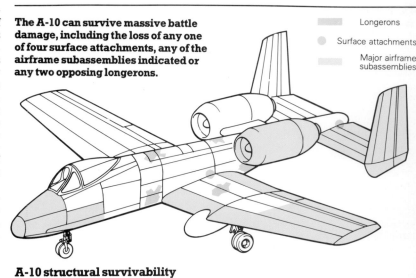

The A-10 can survive massive battle damage, including the loss of any one of four surface attachments, any of the airframe subassemblies indicated or any two opposing longerons.

Longerons
Surface attachments
Major airframe subassemblies

A-10 structural survivability

account in every area of the A-10 design. Important features of the basic configuration include the widely separated engines, the duplicated tail surfaces, and large and powerful controls in all three axes. The combination of these features is intended to allow the A-10 to stay airborne even after sustaining gross airframe damage such as the loss of half the tail assembly, a complete engine or part of the wing.

Internally, the A-10 structure is de-

signed so that any member can be severed by impact without causing a total failure. The wing and the tail surfaces are all designed around three spars of approximately equal size and strength, any two of which can absorb all anticipated air loads. Both the tailplane and the wing are continuous one-piece structures from tip to tip and, as noted above, the landing gear configuration was chosen partly because it eliminated structural breaks in the wing. The fusel-

Above: The effects of 7.62mm armour-piercing projectiles on the bullet-proof/bird-proof front windshield fitted to the A-10.

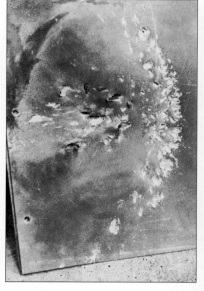

Above: A panel of the armour used for the GAU-8/A ammunition drum after being hit by a 23mm high-explosive projectile during tests.

37mm HE-T
SHOT 5

Above: Further tests were carried out on the titanium armour panels used for the pilot's 'bathtub': the back of one is shown after a 37mm HE hit.

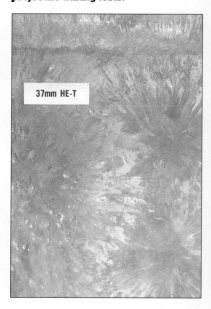

37mm HE-T

Above: The front of the same panel – used for the bathtub side – showing the effects of one 37mm and two 23mm rounds hitting at 90 deg.

age incorporates four main longerons, any three of which can take the full structural loads. Most of the skin area is unstressed, greatly simplifying the repair task.

The structure would have presented no problems had the A-10 been used as it was intended, spending most of its time above the worst turbulence. In Europe, however, the A-10 was routinely flown at high speed and low level for most of its training missions. After cracks began to appear around fastener holes in the lower wing skin (which carries the peak tension loads in high-g flight) the USAF fitted accelerometers to some operational aircraft and found that they were experiencing high g loadings more than three times as often as had been expected. The simplicity of the aircraft, too, means that it spends a great deal of time in the air. A-10s are being fitted with thicker lower wing skins, during routine maintenance, to extend their useful lives to 8,000 hours.

Unique protection
Dealing with the cause of the majority of losses called for action to make the internal components less vulnerable to damage, and to protect them when this was not possible. It is this sort of protection which is unique to the A-10. It exceeds in degree anything applied to any helicopter, with the possible exception of the Mi-24, and is different in nature from the

protection accorded to any fighter aircraft.

The fuel system had proved the weakest spot on the aircraft used in Vietnam. This was, perhaps, not surprising. Self-sealing fuel tanks had been developed before the 1939-45 war; they had an intermediate lining made from a rubber compound, which expanded when a puncture in the inner wall allowed it to be soaked with fuel. They had proved to be a vital feature in com-

Above: Warthog pilots – this one is wearing the badge of the 354th TFW – have expressed great confidence in their aircraft, and they are certainly as well protected as any.

Below: The wide separation of critical systems and control runs, as well as the ready access for maintenance, is apparent in this view of an 81st TFW A-10 in the hangar at RAF Bentwaters/Woodbridge.

bat, but were abandoned in the early 1950s in favour of integral tanks, which were much more efficient and were almost essential to the design of a supersonic fighter with a useful range. It was argued that future air combats would involve missile strikes, which would be lethal regardless of fuel system design, and that jet fuel was less inflammable than the high-octane gasolines used in 1939-45.

In the Vietnam environment, unprotected fuel tanks were as dangerous as ever. Operating altitudes were low, speeds were high, and oxygen-rich air would swirl into any perforation in the airframe, scouring up any fuel leakages in the structural cavities and creating an instantly explosive atmosphere. The high fuel flows of jet engines meant that the fuel would spill more quickly from broken lines.

The A-10 fuel system is fundamentally different from the usual fighter system. For every USAF mission, apart from ferry flights, all the fuel is carried internally. (For ferry purposes, the centreline station and two wing pylons are plumbed, and can each carry a 600US gal (2,271lit) tank.) The 10,700lb (4,853kg) internal tankage is concentrated around the centre-section, so that the vulnerable area presented to hostile weapons is as small as possible, and the fuel lines are short. (This also effectively eliminates trim change with fuel use, making the aircraft simpler and easier to fly.) Most of the fuel is housed in true tanks, rather than integral cells formed by the aircraft skin and structure, although the inner wings include integral tanks.

The tanks are protected in several ways. The fuselage tanks, supplied by the Goodyear Tire & Rubber Company, are tear-resistant, and self-sealing in the event that they are perforated. All the tanks are filled with 'reticulated' rubber foam – that is to say, foam panels folded to fill the tanks. The foam serves several purposes: it slows the spillage of fuel, keeps airflows out of a punctured tank and inhibits the movement of flame fronts through the cavity. Protective firewalls and panels of rigid foam are installed between the individual tanks, and between the tank compartments and the remainder of the airframe, and more foam is fitted between the tanks and the fuselage sides; the object is to prevent any fuel which escapes from the tanks from flooding other airframe cavities.

Fuel provision
Fuel lines and valves are protected, as far as possible, by running them through the tanks. The final stages of the fuel lines are located in the upper section of the fuselage and on top of the engine pylons, where they are protected from damage by the rest of the airframe. The pipes are self-sealing, and the system is fitted with check valves which prevent fuel from flowing into a damaged tank. The single long fuel line leading to the flight-refuelling point in the nose is provided with its own purging system to clean out any remnants of fuel after use. If all else fails, the entire main tank system can be cut off, and two small, self-sealing sump tanks between the engines will provide a 200nm (370km) reserve for a safe return to base.

Equal attention is given to the flight control system, which has some unusual features for a modern combat aircraft. Control signals are transmitted to the hydraulic actuators by cables, rather than rods, because cables are less likely to be jammed by airframe damage. The cable system is duplicated, and either channel can be cut off from the cockpit if it jams. To provide greater protection for the critical pitch and roll axes, the control channels are completely separate from the control surface to the point where they enter the protected cockpit enclosure.

Dual hydraulic systems power the controls in normal operations, but if all power fails, the elevators and rudders can be moved directly by the pilot, through the control cables. Electrically powered trim tabs are fitted to the elevators, and help reduce the considerable control forces needed to fly the A-10 without hydraulic boost. The ailerons are too heavy for direct manual control; instead, if hydraulic power is lost, the control cables move small 'servo-tabs' attached to each aileron, which deflect in the opposite direction to the control input. Aerodynamic forces move the ailerons the other way, creating the desired rolling force. The A-10 is the only Western combat aircraft since the 1950s to be designed with this 'manual reversion' feature.

Each complete control channel runs through one of a pair of accessory tunnels built into opposite sides of the fuselage. These tunnels also carry duplicate hydraulic, electric and pneumatic runs, so that no single hit on one side can deprive the aircraft of any of its services. However, the manual back-up in the control system, and the fact that the landing gear is designed to free-fall into the locked position, means that the A-10 can, in theory, regain its base and land without further damage as long as at least one engine and one flight control channel remain operational.

Conventional systems

Other systems are largely conventional. Each engine powers one of the two 3,000lb/sq in (211kg/m^2) hydraulic circuits, which provide power to the controls, airbrakes, flaps, landing gear, brakes and gun mechanism. Engine bleed air is used for pressurization, air-conditioning and windshield anti-icing and rain clearance (the rest of the airframe is not de-iced) and is also used to clear gases from the gun compartment after firing. A Garrett auxiliary power unit (APU) is installed in a titanium firewall box in the rear fuselage, between the engines, and provides power for engine starting and 'ground loitering'.

The other major areas for specialized protection are in the forward fuselage. One of these is the ammunition drum, which presents a unique potential for catastrophic damage; a single hostile round exploding in the ammunition drum could set off the A-10's magazine and destroy the aircraft instantly. The solution is to provide a layered protection system, designed to protect the drum from the direct impact of an armour-piercing explosive shell. The drum is placed at mid-height in the fuselage, as far from the skin as possible, and is armoured against fragments. The fuselage around it is not armoured in the normal sense, but is provided with trigger plates of various thicknesses to detonate any incoming round, whether armour-piercing, explosive or incendiary, before it reaches the drum.

The pilot himself is protected by a unique structural assembly called 'the bathtub'. This is a bolted-together box, made of heavy titanium sheets – ranging from 0.5in (12.7mm) to 1.5in (38.1mm) in thickness – and built into the forward fuselage, the sides of the box forming the upper sides of the airframe. It extends up to the canopy and windscreen frame, and provides side, front, rear and ventral protection. It accommodates the pilot, on his ejection seat, the flying controls and the instruments.

The sides of the bathtub are intended to defeat a direct hit from a 23mm API shell; the impact is likely to cause 'spalling' or the shedding of titanium frag-

Above: A ground crewman checks the pressure refuelling panel of a 355th TFS, 354th TFW, A-10 prior to takeoff on a training mission.

ments at high velocity from the inner surface of the armour, so the tub is lined internally with layers of ballistic nylon. Weighing some 1,200lb (544kg), the tub is the heaviest single piece of protection in the aircraft. Overall, it is estimated that 2,887lb (1,310kg), or 14 per cent of the A-10's empty weight, goes strictly to protection, without counting the survivability features of the structure and the configuration.

The final layer of protection is provided by the pilot's ejection seat. Initial production A-10s used the then-standard McDonnell Douglas IE-9 Escapac seat, one of the first to feature zero-height, zero-speed capability. However, the same company's ACES II (Advanced Concept Ejection Seat) has since been substituted; it provides better performance, considerably improved pilot comfort (an important factor, given the A-10's long endurance), and is common to the F-15 and F-16.

While it was clearly not practical to verify the effectiveness of the protection system by shooting an A-10 to pieces, the USAF carried out a unique programme of static tests in the course of development. Representative wing and fuselage sections, complete with their fuel loads, were placed on ground rigs and subjected to a 400kt (740km/h) airstream generated by a turbofan engine. Tests with a Soviet 23mm AAA gun, firing API and HEI ammunition – the most dangerous types against fuel cells – demonstrated the fire-suppressing qualities of the foam system around the tanks, and advantages of the foamed tanks. The same weapon was used to evaluate the effectiveness of the titanium armour, in comparison with ceramics and aluminium.

All in all, 707 rounds of 23mm API and HEI were fired at A-10 structural specimens: 430 at the cockpit, 250+ into the fuel tanks, and nearly 60 into the ammunition drum. Among 108 rounds of other calibres were a burst of 7.62mm API fired into the windscreen. It was concluded that the area within which a single 23mm HEI/API strike would be lethal

Above: Studies of aircraft losses over Vietnam showed that a principal cause was the concentration of fuel, hydraulic and electrical systems in small volumes, increasing their vulnerability to a single round: in the A-10 all systems are well protected and widely separated.

Left: Quick turnaround between sorties is vital to the effectiveness of close air support: here an A-10 of the 174th TFW, New York Air National Guard, is supplied with liquid oxygen during Exercise Sentry Castle '81.

Below: Realistic training is an essential part of TAC and reserve force readiness: chemical warfare clothing is worn by an ANG Technical Sergeant of the 104th TFG during an A-10 rescue exercise at Phelps-Collins ANG Base, Michigan.

Bottom: Refuelling an A-10 during Exercise Coronet Sail at Lechfeld AB, Germany. The fuel in the inner wing tanks should be used up by the time an A-10 reaches the battle area, further reducing its vulnerability.

Flight control separation

Aircraft used in Vietnam had duplicate flight control systems, but these were provided to guard against system failure: they were not physically separated, so that a single **hit could disable both primary and back-up systems. The A-10 has duplicate, spatially separated control channels, and a manual back-up, indicated by the broken lines.**

was one-tenth the equivalent area on a smaller, but unhardened, aircraft.

The idea that the A-10 can survive the physical loss of half a wing, half the tail, one engine or all its hydraulics, and even survive several such losses, may appear far-fetched. Consider, though, the case of a certain F-15. The Eagle is a close contemporary of the A-10, and its design drew upon very similar combat experience; while survivability was not a prime requirement in the F-15 design, McDonnell Douglas certainly incorporated many hard lessons from F-4 experience.

In the summer of 1983, an Israeli F-15 was engaged in mock combat with an A-4 when the two aircraft collided. The impact tore off 90 per cent of the Eagle's starboard wing, leaving an 8in (20cm) stump. The A-4 crashed; the Eagle survived thanks to lift from the wide body, survivable hydraulics, jam-resistant control circuits and its powerful tail surfaces. The F-15 was repaired and back in service within weeks.

The tactical value of such toughness is considerable, particularly when it is combined with the structural and systems simplicity of the A-10. Because of

the A-10's design, strikes which might require major repair on another aircraft may simply call for a non-structural patch on the A-10. A heavier hit might destroy a conventional aircraft, but leave the A-10 able to regain its base. An A-10 in such a condition might well be beyond repair, and would almost certainly be too badly damaged to be returned to combat status at a front-line base, but, in wartime, that is not the whole story. The aircraft has recovered its irreplaceable pilot, and now represents a large stockpile of spares; the basic simplicity of the aircraft makes it easier to use the undamaged parts to restore other aircraft to fighting condition.

The A-10's aerodynamic and structural design has proved successful. Like the rest of the weapon system, it accomplishes what it set out to do at the estimated cost. Its design, incomprehensible in terms of pure fighter engineering or aesthetics, represents an uncompromised approach to a clearly defined requirement, and every feature of its gnarled and complex configuration responds to some part of the A-X specification.

Powerplant

In the definition of the A-X programme, the specific requirement which caused most problems was for endurance, or the ability to remain airborne behind the battlefield, ready to deliver a rapid response to any call for support. The reason that it was a problem was that the classic fighter engine is a poor way of providing endurance. The solution was to use a type of engine which had evolved to meet the payload and range requirements of passenger aircraft: the high-bypass-ratio turbofan. The A-10 was and remains unique among combat aircraft in using these inherently efficient and quiet engines.

Jet engines, turbofan engines and propellers all drive in the same way: they seize the air through which the aircraft flies and accelerate it rearwards, and Newton's 'equal and opposite reaction' forces the engine to accelerate forwards. This acceleration is transmitted to the airframe through steel-tube or forged engine mountings, and pulls it through the air.

The difference between the jet and the propeller is that the jet takes a smaller quantity of air, and accelerates it to a much greater degree. The effect on performance and efficiency is fundamental. A good analogy is an oarsman, who is also developing thrust by accelerating a fluid. He rows efficiently when the tips of the oars are almost static in the water with each sweep; he is imparting the smallest possible amount of acceleration to a large mass of water. If he moves his oars twice as fast with the same amount of energy, he will simply move a smaller mass with each stroke. His style will be inelegant and much of his energy will be dissipated in splashes and vortices. The same principle of propulsive efficiency – that the ideal is to apply the minimum acceleration to the maximum mass, disturbing the working fluid as little as possible – applies to aircraft engines.

There is one other basic point to consider. It is impossible for the rower to go faster than he can move the ends of his sculls. When the speed of the boat equals that of the fastest stroke, thrust equals zero. Likewise, each aircraft engine has a theoretical maximum speed at which it will no longer produce thrust – although most have practical speed limits which are lower, for other reasons. At lower speeds, though, the engine will no longer produce thrust equal to its own drag.

Selecting the right type of engine for an aircraft is a matter of defining the desired performance profile, and choosing the type of engine which is best suited to the most critical performance regime. The problem, in the early stages of the A-X programme, was that no engine had yet flown which possessed the desired characteristics.

Jet engine characteristics

The most important attribute of early jet engines was that they could operate at speeds well above the normal limits for propellers. Their main disadvantage was their poor fuel consumption, due to their low pressure ratio – a measure of how much air had to be moved to generate a given amount of power – compared to highly refined piston engines. During the 1950s this disadvantage was reduced by increasing jet pressure ratios through improved high-temperature materials and better compressor design. Higher exhaust velocities went hand-in-hand with increased pressure ratios – the engine drew in less air, squeezed it harder

and expelled it faster. At subsonic speeds, the oars were skating over the water, and the gains in efficiency within the engine were wiped out by propulsive losses.

By the mid-1960s, there were two alternatives to the pure-jet engine. One was the turboprop, in which a high-pressure turbine engine was coupled to a conventional propeller through a power turbine and reduction gearbox. The other was the turbofan engine; this had been created by modifying a pure-jet engine with oversized forward compressor stages. Roughly half the air taken in by the engine 'bypassed' the compressor and turbine. The high-velocity exhaust from the compressor and high-pressure turbine was fed to a second turbine, and drove the fan. The turbofan produced a higher-mass, lower-speed exhaust than the pure jet, and was much more efficient at high subsonic speed: it powered the first jet airliners which could match the range capability of propeller-driven aircraft.

In 1963 the US Navy ordered the LTV A-7, a long-range light attack aircraft designed around a single TF30 turbofan. But this 'low-bypass' engine, although it represented a great advance over the pure-jet, was well out of its element at speeds under 350-400kt (650-740km/h). At higher speeds, fuel flows were too high to provide the endurance needed for the A-X mission.

The turboprop was much better adapted to low-speed cruising, and its maximum speed was acceptable to the USAF. Its disadvantages, outlined in the first chapter, were mainly concerned with the difficulty of integrating two powerful turboprops and their large propellers into a combat aircraft with a wide speed range, and making the resulting aircraft survivable.

Interestingly, a turboprop aircraft in the A-X class had been extensively tested more than a decade before the USAF formulated its requirement. This was the US Navy's Douglas A2D-1 Skyshark, which had started its development life as a turbine-powered version of the A-X's forebear, the Skyraider, and evolved into a different aircraft with a thinner wing and almost exactly the same top speed as the ultimate A-10.

The Skyshark was aimed at achieving twin-engine performance without the engine-out handling problems of a conventional twin. Like some of the early A-X studies, it had two engines deliver-

Below: The General Electric TF34 engine selected for the A-10 was only developed after the original A-X specification had been written.

Right: Originally developed for the US Navy's S-3A, the TF34 was operated for 400 hours under the wing of this B-47 test aircraft.

Right: Originally developed for the US Navy's S-3A, the TF34 was operated for 400 hours under the wing of this B-47 test aircraft.

ing their power along the centreline – the coupled powerplant was the Allison T40, consisting of two T38s with a common gearbox. It was the powerplant that proved the Skyshark's undoing; the Skyshark's designer, Ed Heinemann, likened it to a chronic toothache. One prototype crashed when one turbine unit failed; the dead engine, still coupled to the live powerplant, acted as a huge air pump and drained all the power from the system. Other problems – with the separate engine and propeller control systems, with the reduction gear and overheating of the entire installation – prevented the engine from reaching its projected 5,500shp output.

In 1954 the Skyshark programme was cut back to purely experimental status, and replaced by Heinemann's far simpler Skyhawk. Its significance to the A-X programme lay not only in the similarity of its design goals to those established for the later aircraft, but in the fact that the Skyshark represented the last serious attempt, before A-X, to design a high-performance combat aircraft around turboprop power. The fundamental problem, as before, would be to steer a path between the conventional twin-turboprop installation, with its drag, weight and engine-out-condition penalties, and the risks and complexity of some type of coupled layout. The latter offered better performance, but it would be hard to ensure or demonstrate that it would not be vulnerable to a single hit.

High-bypass turbofans

The arrival of the classic compromise, the high-bypass turbofan, was entirely unexpected; neither of the engines eventually tested under the A-X programme had been designed with it in mind. The concept originated independently with several manufacturers in the early 1960s. Rolls-Royce and Pratt & Whitney approached it through extrapolation from their existing large commercial engines. Lycoming saw it as a means to break into the fixed-wing turbine power market, making the maximum use of its existing T55 turbine engine; the company was the first to run a true high-bypass engine, in late 1963.

General Electric's route into the market was different again. In the late 1950s GE had started work on a design for a vertical takeoff fighter using lift fans. These resembled enlarged jet engine rotors, and were designed to be buried within the wing of a small aircraft; they were driven by exhaust from small jet engines, impinging on small turbine blades fixed to the outside of the lift fan.

Very early in the 1960s the lift-fan research spawned a demonstration programme for a cruise fan – essentially, a lift fan turned through 90deg to give propulsive thrust. The biggest test rig comprised an 80in (205cm) fan driven by the exhaust of a J79. Results showed that the big fan could operate at high subsonic speeds with much greater efficiency than previous turbofans. Data from these tests was passed to the USAF in 1962, while the service was in the early stages of formulating its requirement for a huge strategic freighter.

In 1962-63, GE moved from the cruise fan, in which the fan and the gas generator were separate, to a more integrated concept in which the fan was driven by a conventional turbine, via a shaft running through the engine. Up to eight times as much air passed through the fan as went through the compressor, combustor and turbines (the 'core engine'); that was to say, the engine had an 8:1 bypass ratio.

This was the basis for the GE1/6 demonstrator engine, the foundation for GE's August 1965 victory in the contest to provide power for the USAF's new C-5.

This early experience and background set the pattern for GE high-bypass engines. GE's fortunes in jet propulsion had been founded on the J79, a single-shaft engine with a large number of stages and a great deal of internal variable geometry, and its later turbojet engines featured similar configurations. Its new high-bypass fan engines sustained the family tradition. They had long, many-staged 'cores', resembling GE's single-shaft turbojets, with the fan added to the front and the fan turbine at the rear. Unlike its rivals' engines, GE's big-fan engines did not have low-pressure compressors, although one or two 'booster' stages might be attached to the fan shaft behind the fan.

While GE's heavy brigade worked on the TF39 for the C-5, the company's small-engine group at Lynn, Massachusetts, was looking at smaller high-bypass engines. As Lycoming had done, GE started with a proven turbine core; the first high-bypass test engine built at Lynn was based on a T64 turboshaft engine, fitted with a scaled-down version of the TF39 fans and a new multi-stage power turbine. Otherwise, the geometry was unchanged. There was no booster stage, although the overall pressure ratio was slightly increased by the presence of the fan stage.

The existence of engines such as the Lycoming and GE demonstrators was to bring about a decisive change in the A-X programme. The new engines were not as efficient as turboprops in the A-X speed range, but they had many other advantages. They were easier to install; with no propellers, they could be located close to the centreline where engine-out

Above: The TF34 test installation on the Navy's B-47, with the associated wiring runs carried along the leading edge of the wing.

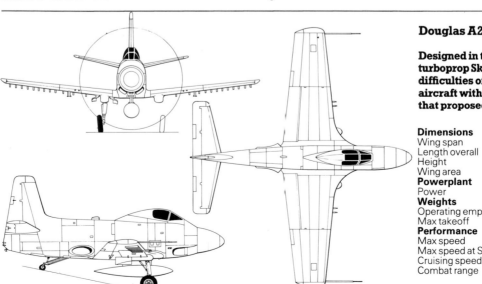

Douglas A2D-1 Skyshark

Designed in the early 1950s, the twin-turboprop Skyshark illustrated the difficulties of using such engines in an aircraft with performance similar to that proposed for the A-X.

Dimensions	
Wing span	50ft 2in (15.28m)
Length overall	41ft 2in (12.54m)
Height	17ft (5.18m)
Wing area	400sq ft (37.2m²)
Powerplant	Allison XT40-A-2
Power	5,500shp (4,105kW)
Weights	
Operating empty	12,994lb (5,894kg)
Max takeoff	21,764lb (9,872kg)
Performance	
Max speed	435kt (806km/h)
Max speed at SL	406kt (752km/h)
Cruising speed	249kt (461km/h)
Combat range	553nm (1,024km)
	at 320kt (593km/h)

Above: The first DT & E A-10 was the first to have the USAF-standard TF34-100, the prototypes having flown with US Navy engines.

Below: TF34 cutaway, showing the single-stage fan, 14-stage compressor derived from GE's T64, and high- and low-pressure turbines.

Right: A-10s with external tanks form up before a ferry mission. Despite doubts in some quarters about the advisability of using a high-bypass turbofan on a combat aircraft, the high mounting keeps the intakes well clear of runway debris, and upward-pointing exhausts reduce the risk of FOD in a stream takeoff.

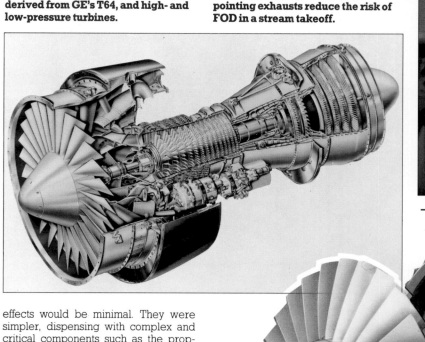

Below: The five basic modular components of the TF34: (from left) titanium-blade fan and casing; axial compressor; annular combustor of

effects would be minimal. They were simpler, dispensing with complex and critical components such as the propeller and reduction gear. (While the Lycoming engine did have a reduction gear, it had a much smaller ratio than a turboprop's gear and was much less complicated.) All in all, their advantages were overwhelming.

While the A-X requirement was still being refined, the US Navy followed a similar line of reasoning, and specified high-bypass turbofans for its new VSX – the replacement for the S-2 Tracker carrier-based antisubmarine warfare aircraft. GE based its proposed VSX engine on data from the test engine run at Lynn, although it would be a basically different engine from the T64. In late 1966 the Navy awarded design contracts for the GE engine, now designated TF34, and the Allison TF32, and definitive proposals were submitted in January 1968. In April GE was announced the winner, and Lockheed was awarded the contract to build the S-3A airframe. According to a GE official history, the victory came as a complete surprise to many of those associated with the programme.

Development of the TF34 moved ahead smoothly, and the engine made its first run in May 1969. In January 1971 it started a 200-hour test programme beneath the port wing of an obsolete Boeing B-47 bomber, leased by GE as a test-bed and operated from the company's flight test centre at Edwards AFB. Meanwhile, development of the S-3A Viking proceeded smoothly, and the compact ASW aircraft made its first flight in January 1972; the engine was qualified for US Navy use in August of that year.

There were several factors favouring the TF34 over any other engine proposed in the A-X competition. The most important was that the development of the engine, and initial production, were already fully funded under the S-3A programme, and USAF development expenditures would be confined to any changes needed for the A-X mission; none of these would be fundamental, whereas the production version of the Lycoming F102 would combine a higher-powered core, based on the T55-L-11B, with a redesigned fan. The TF34 was also at the beginning of its development life, and GE had identified a series of changes which could make extra thrust available if it were needed. The USAF

already planned to use eight TF34s to power the new airborne warning and control system (Awacs) under development by Boeing, so there was some potential for commonality. Lastly, GE was an established supplier of combat engines to the USAF (unlike Lycoming, for instance) and already had the facilities and resources to develop the A-X engine.

GE's main disadvantage was cost. The TF34 was not a particularly simple engine, and had been developed for a quite demanding Navy mission; it would cost almost $140,000 more than the proposed production version of the Lycoming F102. (Both Fairchild and Northrop were required to provide data for both en-

gines in their final proposals to the USAF, so in that sense the two engines were in direct competition.) However, it proved possible to reduce the cost of the TF34 by eliminating some features which were unnecessary for the A-X mission, and the GE engine emerged victorious.

Since that time, the TF34 has done steady rather than spectacular business for GE. Just after the A-10 decision was announced, Boeing and the USAF decided to use the older TF33-P-7 for the Awacs, to save the cost of developing a new version of the TF34 and its twin nacelle. Production of 187 S-3A Vikings ended in 1978, and A-10 production has also ceased. The basic engine is now in low-rate production in a commercially

Above: Large access doors allow the TF34 to be maintained 'on condition', removal of modules only being necessary when a problem arises.

Below: Ladders are needed to reach the engines, but the pod mounting makes them readily accessible when the access doors are opened.

nickel alloy with low-pressure fuel injection system; two-stage high-pressure tubine; and four-stage low-pressure turbine.

certified version, the CF34, for the Canadair Challenger 601 business jet, and a marine turboshaft version, the LM500, has been demonstrated.

An engine *aficionado* would immediately recognise the TF34 as a GE engine. There is no low-pressure compressor, although incoming air is slightly compressed by the fan before being split into bypass and core flows. The mechanical layout of the compressor is similar to that of the T64, with 14 axial stages, and the stators, or static blades, in the first five stages can be varied in pitch. Variable stators were developed by GE for the J73 and J79, and their use in large numbers is a GE trademark. Their function is to vary the airflow through the engine, making it easier to start a single high-pressure-ratio spool and improving handling; other manufacturers generally split such a long compressor into two spools. The compressor is driven by a conventional two-stage turbine.

Titanium fan blades
Aerodynamically, the fan is based on TF39 technology, although the design is modified to cater for the lower bypass ratio of the TF34 – 6:1, versus 8:1 for the C-5 engine – and does not feature the complex and unique one-and-a-half-stage configuration of the TF39. The fan has a single stage, with no booster stage. Each blade is forged and machined to shape from a solid piece of titanium alloy,

the only material available at that time with sufficient lightness, tensile strength and rigidity to meet the requirements of a high-bypass engine.

Mechanically, the fan was different from that of the TF39. Because of its smaller size, it was not necessary to brace the blades by linking them together, so the annular mid-span shroud could be eliminated. The TF34 is also designed so that each blade can be removed individually by pulling out a securing pin, rotating the fan and withdrawing the blade through a slot in the fan case. The fan is driven by a conventional four-stage turbine.

Perhaps the most technically important feature of the TF34, at the time of its appearance, was the combustor section. Previous combustors had comprised sheet metal assemblies, called 'liners', built into the engine case. These promoted good combustion, and were cheap; the snag was that they had limited lives and needed frequent maintenance, and any work on the combustor called for dismantling the entire engine. The TF34, however, was the first engine to feature a more durable combustor, which was machined from a nickel alloy originally developed for turbine blades.

The TF34's fuel-injection system was also novel, relying on a two-stage swirler to generate powerful aerodynamic shearing forces which would vaporize the fuel before ignition. While these caused development problems in late 1971, they were fixed before they could delay the entire programme, and the Navy engine was qualified on schedule.

Later in the decade, GE's advanced combustor technology was to be a major factor in the success of its F404 and F110 fighter engines. Not only did the combustor prove efficient and durable, but the injector/burner system proved to be virtually free of visible smoke emission. GE, of course, had good reasons for working in this area: not for nothing was the twin-J79-powered F-4 nicknamed

'Ol' Smokey'. Smokeless exhaust is a tactically important feature of the A-10.

Modular maintenance
The TF34 is one of the first service engines to be designed with easy maintenance as a major consideration. It is a 'modular' engine, designed so that the main mechanical components can be separated from each other without disconnecting and stripping all the accessories. All the compressor blades can be individually removed and replaced by opening the engine carcass – which is split along the the centreline – without dismantling the entire engine. The TF34 is also supplied with strategically located borescope ports, which allow the mechanic to insert a fibre-optic probe and survey the engine's interior for damage while it is still 'on the wing' (although that expression does not apply to the A-10).

Generally, the TF34 is designed to be maintained 'on condition': that is to say, the engine is only removed or serviced when regular performance checks, metal chip detectors in the oil system, or external and borescope inspections indicate that there is a problem. If the difficulty can be traced to a given module, it can be replaced without removing the engine from service, and, in some cases, without pulling the engine off the aircraft. (In the case of the A-10, though, it is probably easier to bring the engine down to ground level.) This is a great advance on earlier engines, which had to be removed, disassembled and inspected every few hundred hours, the intervals being determined on the basis of service experience.

Approaching the A-X competition, the GE engineers determined that they could easily match the opposition on performance, but were vulnerable to price comparisons. There was little point, therefore, in making changes to the basic aerodynamic and thermodynamic characteristics of the engine, which

Above: A 355th TFW A-10 makes a low pass over the Gila Bend range, Arizona. The turbofan's high thrust at low speeds formed the key to the A-10's low-level manoeuvrability.

Left: A Warthog touches down on the runway. Landing distance, even at maximum weight, is an economical 2,500ft (762m), while a fully-loaded A-10 can take off in 4,500ft (1,372m).

Right: A-10s of the 917th TFW refuelling from a 78th Air Refuelling Squadron KC-10 during an AFRES Aerials exercise held at Carswell AFB, Texas, in September 1983.

would accomplish little in terms of useful performance and add to the overall cost of the engine to the USAF. Instead, GE concentrated on cutting the manufacturing cost of the engine, without making extensive changes that would add to its development cost.

The only mission-related changes to the TF34 for the A-X concerned its installation. Even these were quite small. The main thrust and support bearings for the engine remained on top, as they had been designed for the S-3A's underwing engine installation; in the A-10, the engines were to be hung from dual forged outriggers projecting from the top of the fuselage. Some accessories were moved, to facilitate maintenance and satisfy the USAF requirement for left-to-right interchangeability.

The engine installation itself was conventional, except for the near-full length fan cowlings, the first on a high-bypass engine. They were chosen so that the exhaust nozzles could be angled slightly upwards, reducing changes of trim with changes of engine power. The engines were set higher than was ideal for maintenance purposes; by way of compensation, the cowlings, including the inner wall of the fan duct, were split and top-hinged, providing easy access to most of the engine without removing a single component. Provisions for hoisting the engines were built into the engine mounts, eliminating the need for external lifting devices.

Most of the differences between the Navy and USAF engines were the result of GE's effort to identify and implement savings in production costs. These were possible because the USAF requirement was, in some ways, less severe than that of the USN. The S-3, for example, was required to loiter for long periods at low speed in icing conditions. Because of the low speed the engines would not be at maximum power, and the icing bleed air would be cooler than normal. The Navy

TF34 needed a complex, large-volume de-icing system to cope with these conditions; the USAF, however, had no icing requirement for the A-X, and the entire system could be eliminated.

Another specific Navy requirement was to operate at low thrust, but with high power being drawn from the engine to feed the S-3A's complex systems; draining power from the compressor caused aft-end temperatures to rise higher than they would on the A-X, at least in sustained operation. In some cases, it proved possible to use cheaper materials for the A-X engine. Other changes simply involved eliminating machining operations such as the removal of excess material and the drilling of lightening holes, trading a slight weight increase for lower cost. The USAF engine also required, and received, a simpler and cheaper control system.

The first YA-10s flew with Navy-standard development engines. The modified USAF engine, designated TF34-GE-100, made its first run in July 1973. Production-configured engines were put through 2,181 hours of testing on GE and USAF ground-testing facilities, including two 150-hour endurance cycles. The engine was declared qualified for military use in November 1974, and flew on the first pre-production A-10 early in the following year.

Reliability in service
The TF34 has posed few problems in development and service, and had logged two million flight hours by the end of 1982. The service environment has been more strenuous than was envisaged at the start of the programme, mainly because the lower-flying, higher-energy tactics now used keep the engines close to their full-power ratings much of the time. Largely for this reason, hot-section wear and tear has caused some 10 per cent of TF34s to need main-base overhaul and repair only 500 hours after

being rebuilt in the field. To correct this particular situation, A-10 powerplants were up-graded to the new TF34-GE-100A model by the introduction of a modified combustor and high-pressure turbine module.

The most important change was the introduction of 'directionally solidified' DSR80 material in the first-stage turbine blades. DS blades are cast in a special furnace and are allowed to cool from the root to the tip. The metal forms long, uniform crystals instead of a random crystal structure: this means that some of the elements in a conventional casting alloy, which are added to bond the crystal boundaries and which are otherwise undesirable, can be removed. The DSR blades are more costly to produce than conventional blades, but the longer life more than makes up for the cost difference.

The -100A update included a number of other changes: combustor modifications, to reduce 'hot spots' in the gas flow striking the turbine, changes to shrouds and seals and other new materials. The hot-section life of the -100A should be 2,000 hours, including 360 hours at maximum power, both figures being twice those attained by the -100 engine. The TF34-GE-100A was qualified for service in August 1983.

The TF34 has proved resistant to foreign-object damage (FOD) in service, despite those who doubted the wisdom of using a high-bypass engine on a combat-type aircraft. The high engine mounting keeps the inlets well clear of runway FOD, while the high exhaust position and upward-pointing exhaust reduce the problems of FOD in a stream takeoff. In 1982, A-10s involved in exercises in Egypt flew through heavy sandstorms with no problems, and the engines did not even need to be washed. Neither has the A-10 suffered unduly from birdstrikes, even in Northern Europe.

Above: Post-flight inspection of an A-10's TF34. The titanium fan blades have proved highly resistant to bird strikes over Europe, and have shrugged off heavy sandstorms during exercises in Egypt.

Non-problems are rarely investigated, but the most likely reason for the toughness of the TF34 lies in its basic front-end layout. The fan itself, with solid titanium blades and a modest 7,800rpm speed, is unlikely to suffer much damage from a birdstrike. The inlet to the core, where FOD can do far more damage, is not very prominent, being flush with the inner wall of the duct, and is well behind the fan. If a bird hits the fan, the heavier fragments will be thrown outwards, well clear of the core inlet. The same applies for any objects denser than the inlet air, including sand and water. Some other high-bypass engines, which have encountered more serious problems with ingestion and erosion, feature core inlets immediately behind the fan.

Operating their engines at constant full power in combat, A-10 pilots have

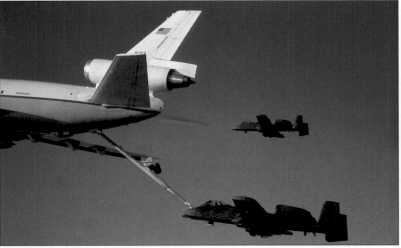

Below: A fuel tank is fitted under the wing of an A-10 in JAWS (Joint Attack Weapon System) colour scheme ready for deployment to Europe in 1978.

Above: Even without air refuelling, the A-10 has a ferry range of 2,240nm (4,148km) with a 20min reserve against 50kt (93km/h) headwinds.

Above: the unusual nose position for the refuelling receptable proved to be an improvement on the more normal location to the rear of the cockpit.

encountered no serious handling problems. In 1980 some engine stalls were being reported during prolonged gun-firing; this is understandable, since the GAU-8/A spits out 24lb (10.9kg) of used propellant every second when firing at its maximum rate. Usually this is not too much of a problem operationally: there are few targets which can absorb more than a short burst from the A-10's multi-barrelled cannon.

Another feature of the TF34 is that it is inherently much quieter than any other fighter engine. The advantage of this attribute in the tactical arena may be in dispute, but it has certainly been welcome to the people in the neighbour-hood of the A-10's operating bases in Europe, and must be some comfort to the Warthog's groundcrews.

A higher-powered version of the TF34 was to have been developed for the Awacs programme, and would have improved A-10 performance in some respects, but GE's plans for uprated engines have not yet been implemented. Using the same fan as the existing version, the TF34 could be taken up to 10,000lb (4,540kg) thrust by increasing the turbine entry temperature; the standard core, mated to a larger fan and operating at the same temperatures, would yield around 11,500lb (5,100kg) thrust. Despite this improved performance, there is no current requirement for an engine in this class, however.

Engine change proposal

Briefly, in 1976, alternative engines were studied for the A-10, in an effort to generate more interest in the A-10 among Western European customers. Although the European F-16 programme was under way by that time, the Tornado was still several years away from service and its future was by no means assured. The prevailing view among western European air forces was that the A-10 was too slow, and that airborne loiter was, in European conditions and potential tactical situations, both a costly and unnecessary manoeuvre. Fairchild therefore investigated a version of the A-10 in which some endurance would be traded for higher speed by installing different engines.

At the 1976 Farnborough Air Show Fairchild showed a model of an A-10 with longer, slimmer cowlings, and suggested that the aircraft could be powered by unreheated versions of two current fighter engines: General Electric's own J101, a very-low-bypass engine developing more than 10,000lb (4,540kg), and Europe's Turbo-Union RB.199. Either engine would generate more net thrust than the TF34 at higher airspeeds, and the modified aircraft would have been some 30-50kt (55-93km/h) faster than the standard A-10 in level flight, with weapons carried. The A-10's airframe limit of 450kt (830km/h) was, however, too slow for the taste of European air force commanders, who continued to regard the A-10 as too highly specialised in its combat role, and something of a curiosity. No serious discussions took place as a result.

The engines of the A-10 are unique among the world's fighter and attack aircraft, and the key to its unusual performance in both the areas of endurance and manoeuvrability. Their basic configuration is more akin to the typical modern airliner engine than to the normal fighter powerplant: for the mission which the A-10 was designed to perform, though, they are ideal.

Left: An A-10 of the 174th TFW, New York Air National Guard, its refuelling panel open, is de-iced with warm air during a deployment to Lechfeld AB, Germany, in 1981.

Weapons and Avionics

No other aircraft approaches the A-10 in its ability to carry a heavy load of hard-target ordnance; a single Warthog can carry enough weaponry to disable 16 main battle tanks. The primary weapon, unique to the A-10, is the massive GAU-8/A Avenger Gatling cannon, and this powerful gun is backed up by the highly accurate fire-and-forget Maverick missile, which offers a choice of television, scene-magnification TV and infrared guidance. With these weapons the A-10 accomplishes its mission without the need for sophisticated – and costly and unreliable – weapon-aiming avionics. Meanwhile, the navigation and ECM systems have been upgraded as a result of operational experience.

If the infantry commander has one recurrent nightmare, it is the unexpected rumble of armour. It signifies that he is about to be engaged by a force which his defensive weapons may blunt, but which they will probably not neutralize, and that it is too late to call for friendly armour to support his unit. In a ground-only battle, the options are immediate retreat, or destruction.

The nightmare came true more than once in Vietnam, and it can happen to a front-line unit at almost any time, even

Below: 354th TFW ground crew prepare to reload a GAU-8/A's ammunition drum, using the Ammunition Loading System.

with the best reconnaissance and intelligence. Its importance for the A-10 is that it represents the most critical test for close air support (CAS). Only air power can rescue the unit under attack, and it can do so only if it arrives quickly, can distinguish friend and enemy, and can engage and defeat the attackers. This leads to a few basic requirements for effective CAS.

It can be taken for granted that the CAS aircraft will be outnumbered by main battle tanks (MBTs) and their escorts and support vehicles. Almost by definition, the CAS aircraft is responding to an emergency, and there will be no time to muster a superior force. The first essential for an effective CAS system is

the ability to kill several targets in a single sortie.

The primary target is the MBT, a notoriously difficult machine to kill. Its resistance to blast weapons is sufficient to make their use uneconomical, and light cluster weapons, dispensing a shower of submunitions over a wide area, are also ineffective. Another basic requirement for CAS, therefore, is an airborne weapon that can guarantee a direct, lethal hit on a tank under operational conditions. Modern armoured formations, particularly in Soviet practice, carry their own defensive systems, so the weapon must have sufficient range to be fired from a position of relative security. Finally, even the fastest-

Above: The 9,000lb (40kN) recoil thrust of the GAU-8/A cannon demanded a centreline location, and the forward fuselage was designed around the gun and its ammunition.

responding CAS may not reach the fight before the attacking armour has engaged the friendly force. Telling friend from foe, when the position of the target is no help, is a great deal more difficult than simply acquiring, tracking and shooting a target which is known to be hostile.

General Electric GAU-8/A Avenger 30mm armament system

Easily the biggest gun carried by any combat aircraft, the GAU-8/A is based on General Electric's proven range of Gatling type cannon. The ammunition drum holds 1,350 rounds which are forced into the feed chute by the rotary motion of the helical inner drum. Each of the seven barrels has its own breech and bolt, with integral firing and locking mechanism, and as a round is fed into the breech the bolt rams it home and locks. The firing pin is compressed by a cocking pin and released by a trigger; after firing, the bolt is unlocked and withdraws the empty cartridge case, which is returned to the ammunition drum. As in the original Gatling, the rotation of the barrels and their individual firing mechanisms on a single rotor synchronize the firing sequence through a system of cam tracks on the inside of the rotor casing, though hydraulic power is used rather than the manual crank of its nineteenth-century ancestor.

GAU-8/A ammunition

Aluminium nose

Steel body **Training practice**

Heavy metal penetrator — Aluminium positioning ring

Aluminium base — Steel windscreen

Armour-piercing incendiary

Right and below: The three basic types of GAU-8/A ammunition. All use aluminium cartridge cases, giving a substantial weight saving, and plastic driving bands for extended barrel life; the API round is produced in two slightly different versions.

Igniter tube — Aluminium cartridge case — Plastic rotating bands

High-explosive/incendiary mix

Steel fragmenting body

M505A3 impact fuze

Single base nitrocellulose extruded propellant or double base nitrocellulose/nitroglycerine ball propellant

High-explosive/incendiary

Looking at these basic requirements in the mid-1960s, the USAF planners realised that there was no combination of weapons and sensors in the inventory, or even envisaged, which could meet the requirement. Unguided weapons and iron bombs were not accurate at safe ranges. Autonomous air-to-surface missiles guided by TV cameras were under study, but even if they worked as advertised, they would not kill a tank with every shot (the air-to-air battles over Vietnam had been a cold shower for those who believed in theoretical kill probabilities, as defined in the early 1960s). The cost-per-kill numbers, placed against the relatively low cost of the cheap, unrefined Soviet MBT, were not encouraging.

Reviewing the history of aircraft-versus-tank battles in the 1939-45 war, the USAF came across a few successes for the aircraft. Most of these involved the use of a heavy-calibre gun: the British Hurricane IID in the North African desert, with its two 40mm cannon; the German Ju 87G, with two 37mm weapons; and the Soviet Il-2, with 23mm or 37mm cannon. There was also the German Hs 129, with its massive 75mm gun, designed to tackle the huge Josef Stalin MBT.

The gun became the standard weapon of the A-X by a process of elimination: there was simply no other weapon in sight that could kill a tank from a fast-moving aircraft at a reasonable cost. The encouraging lesson from history, and from experience and tests with the more modern 30mm calibre weapons used by Britain and France, was that a tank could be destroyed by an airborne gun of moderate calibre, because the aircraft could attack the more lightly armoured sides and top of the tank. The tanks of the 1960s were a great deal better protected than those of the 1940s, but the design of guns, and, to a greater extent, the design of ammunition, had made advances as well.

Gun design

The design of an airborne anti-tank cannon had barely been considered since the mid-1940s. The principles of gun design, though, are constant regardless of the intended use of the weapon. Since the modern gun was conceived, in the mid-1880s, these principles have become fairly well established.

The gun has been likened to a piston engine, with the barrel as the cylinder and the shell as the piston. Its power is proportional to the pressure generated by the expansion of the burning gases inside the barrel, and there are physical and practical limits, such as gun strength and durability, to that pressure. The power of the gun, and the speed of the shell, can be increased by adding more propellant without increasing calibre. But if the peak pressure is to be held constant, the propellant gases must have more time, and more room, to expand. This means a longer barrel, and is the reason why the ratio of barrel length to calibre is a basic parameter in gun design.

The speed of the shell – muzzle velocity – is a contributor to absolute range, but it is a vital quality in two specific types of gunnery. These, conveniently, are airborne gunnery and shooting tanks.

In airborne gunnery accuracy is the main requirement. No system, including a gun, is absolutely consistent in operation. Rounds may vary – to a tiny degree – in the burning rate of their propellant. Firing from a warm barrel is not quite the same as firing from a cold barrel. Outside the barrel, the weight of the shell and the wind take effect, and cause the shell to deviate from the straight and narrow path. An added factor in an aircraft is the varying speed and g loading when the gun is fired. All these add up to 'dis-

Right: Hand-loading 30mm rounds for early firing trials with the GAU-8/A. Each round is 11.4in (290mm) long, and the complete API round weighs an impressive 2.05lb (930g).

persion', the fact that shells diverge slightly in flight. Dispersion cannot be eliminated, but most of the factors that cause it are reduced by higher muzzle velocity.

The importance of velocity to antitank gunnery is in the nature of the target. Tanks are invulnerable to blast explosives, except in extremely large quantities. The common feature of all antitank munitions is that they concentrate their force on a single point, either in the form of a solid piece of hard metal or, in the case of a hollow-charge warhead, as a high-velocity jet of vaporized metal. The hollow charge is too bulky to be fired from a gun; the effectiveness of the solid penetrator is proportional to its impact velocity, and thus to its muzzle velocity.

Finally, antitank and airborne gunnery share a common feature. The fighter or attack pilot has neither the means nor the time to consider the ballistic drop of the shell with distance, and it is certainly impractical to fire and observe a ranging shot before firing for effect. While it may be possible for a ground-based antitank gun to fire a ranging shot before engaging a tank, it is definitely inadvisable. The effective range, in both cases, is the maximum range at which ballistic drop can be ignored: 'point-blank' shooting, in the original and accurate sense of the term. This range is almost directly proportional to muzzle velocity.

Given the basic principles of gun design and gunnery, and the state of the art

in projectile design and propellant composition, the shape of the A-X gun became a factor of the operational requirements. These could be summarized as the need to assure the destruction of a T-62 tank at 4,000ft (1,200m) range. However, the phrase 'assure the destruction' introduced a new parameter into the requirement: rate of fire.

High muzzle velocity could reduce dispersion, but not eliminate it, particularly in airborne firing. It was reasonable to expect the new gun to put half its shots within an approximately tank-sized area from a given point at maximum effective range. The problem was that no two shells would be fired from the same point, because the aircraft would be moving. Again, this was a factor which could never be eliminated. It could, however, be reduced. The key was a very high rate of fire, so that the movement of the firing point between each round would be as small as possible.

The requirement for the A-X gun took shape in 1968-69. It soon became clear that the weapon would be of awesome size, and would utterly dwarf any aircraft gun since the 75mm freaks of 1939-45. Its shells would be more than twice as heavy as those of any gun with a comparable muzzle velocity or rate of fire, and the rest of the weapon would naturally grow in proportion. The multiple-target-kill capability required by the USAF, together with the high rate of fire, also meant that the A-X would carry more

rounds of its heavy ammunition than other aircraft.

The rate of fire demanded by the USAF determined the basic configuration of the gun. It would be a design which dated back two decades or a century, depending on your historical perspective. It was in 1861 that Richard Jordan Gatling patented the first operable machine gun, a weapon which could load, cock and fire itself at a far faster

rate than any human operator could attain. The Gatling gun consisted of six independent barrels and breeches, arranged in a circle and revolving around a common axis under the power of a hand crank, and it was used in the American Civil War, and later by the British Army. Its limitation was its need for external power, and by the turn of the century it had been replaced by weapons such as the Maxim, which used

Range estimation

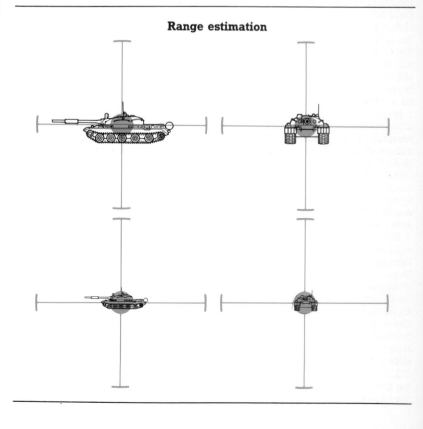

Above: The GAU-8/A expels 24lb (10.9kg) of used propellant a second, causing occasional engine stalls, but few targets can withstand more than a very short burst.

Below: An M48 on the receiving end of a burst of fire from the GAU-8/A: as the rounds penetrate the tank armour, ammunition and fuel inside ignite to cause secondary explosions.

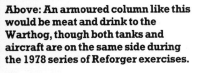

Above: An armoured column like this would be meat and drink to the Warthog, though both tanks and aircraft are on the same side during the 1978 series of Reforger exercises.

recoil energy to operate the mechanism.

The Gatling remained a museum piece until 1946, when the US Army Air Force began serious investigations of a new type of aircraft gun. In 1939-45 German aircraft cannon had proved superior in most respects to the Anglo-French Hispano, and vastly more effective than the USAAF's standard .5in (12.7mm) machine gun. The invading Allies also discovered prototypes of the Mauser MG 213 revolver cannon, which could fire twice as fast as any previous weapon for a modest increase in weight.

Post-war development of aircraft guns followed two parallel tracks. The development of the MG 213 was completed independently in Britain, France and the USA. The other route was started by the USAAF, which intended to create an ultimate aircraft gun, combining high velocity with an unheard-of rate of fire: the aim was to arm a fighter or defend a bomber with a single gun.

This was Project Vulcan, and a development contract was awarded to General Electric's Armament Systems Department in 1946. GE's response to the USAAF requirement was to resurrect the Gatling. There were a number of reasons for this apparent throwback to the past. The most important was that the Gatling, coupled with a modern-technology feed system, could reach and sustain otherwise unthinkable rates of fire. The MG 213, firing at 1,400rds/min, was close to the limits on barrel life and barrel heating. A six-barrel Gatling, by contrast,

could fire at 6,000rds/min, but each barrel would be firing at little more than two-thirds the rate of the MG 213 barrel.

The Gatling's need for external power was no longer a problem, now that fighter aircraft carried their own reliable electrical power supplies; in fact, it could be seen as a positive advantage. While a recoil-powered gun might run out of power if a round failed to fire, the Gatling's external power provided a number of options for clearing a misfired round from the cycle. A final mechanical advantage of the Gatling was that many of its functions were driven by the rotary movement of the barrel assembly; rotary movements are inherently more reliable, and impose fewer loads on the rest of the system, than the reciprocating motions of a conventional gun.

GE ground-tested its first T-171 20mm Gatling in 1949, successfully firing up to 6,000rds/min. The cannon's only real drawback was its unusual, bulky shape, which made it very difficult to install in an aircraft not specifically designed to carry it; it did not enter service until early 1958, first on the Lockheed F-104 and later on the Republic F-105, under the military designation M61A1. It proved its worth on the F-105 over North Vietnam, was squeezed into the nose of the F-4, packed into the USAF A-7 and fired in broadsides from AC-119 and AC-130 gunships. GE had developed a 7.62mm baby Gatling, the Minigun, which was fitted to helicopters, AC-47 'Puff-Ships' and the A-37B. By the time the A-X requirement emerged, the USAF was thoroughly convinced of the merits of the Gatling.

The fact that GE had designed every operational Gatling gun in the world gave it something of a head start in the

succeeding competition. The company's own efforts at research and development, aimed at expanding its family of Gatling weapons, also told in its favour; a six-barrel, 30mm demonstrator designated T-212 was tested in 1967-68, before the formal USAF requirement was issued. As outlined in the first chapter, the contest to produce the GAU-8/A weapon for the A-10 led to a 'shoot-off' between rival prototypes from GE and Philco-Ford, which had developed the MG 213-based M39 for the F-100 and F-5. GE was announced the winner in mid-1973, and the production cannon was first fired from the A-10 in 1975.

GAU-8/A Avenger

The GAU-8/A Avenger is more than a scaled-up M61. Such a weapon could have been designed and built, but would have been unacceptably heavy. The first of many design differences is that the heavier weapon has seven barrels, instead of six. The maximum firing rate is lower (4,200rds/min versus 6,000), and the firing rate per barrel is lower again; each GAU-8/A barrel fires a maximum of 10rds/sec, while the M61 barrel fires nearly 17. Essentially, maximum firing rate has been traded for a heavier, more accurate and more lethal round; each shell is far heavier than the M50 round fired by the older weapon, and the more modest firing rate per barrel is necessary to ensure a long barrel life. The USAF specified a minimum 21,000-round life for each set of barrels. The GAU-8/A also has an improved and more compact bolt design which reduces the overall length and weight of the gun. The GAU-8/A is relatively compact, being only fractionally larger in diameter than the much less powerful M61.

The basic GAU-8/A gun closely follows the philosophy of Richard Gatling's original. Each of the seven 30mm barrels is a simple non-repeating rifle, with its own breech and bolt; the cocking and firing mechanism is built into the bolt. The bolt rams the shell into the breech and locks into position; a cocking pin compresses the firing spring, and a trigger releases it. The bolt is unlocked, and slides back to withdraw the empty cartridge case.

None of the barrels, though, can fire without some force to move and lock the bolt, and cock and release the trigger. The genius of the original Gatling concept is that all these operations are carried out and synchronized through the movement of a single component: the multiple barrels, built into one rotating assembly (which GE calls the 'rotor') and revolving on a common axis inside the gun casing. The firing mechanisms for each individual barrel are located on the outside of the rotor, and engage fixed cam tracks on the inside of the casing. As the rotor spins, the curving cam tracks engage and move the bolt, the locking mechanism and the firing pin, and take the barrel through a complete, perfectly synchronized firing sequence for each revolution of the rotor. This, essentially, is what happens in all the GE weapons.

Each GAU-8/A barrel is some 80 calibres in length. The muzzle velocity of the GAU-8/A is about the same as that of the M61, but the heavier, more advanced ammunition is not only more destructive but has better ballistic properties. It decelerates much less rapidly after leaving the barrel, so that its time of flight to 4,000ft (1,200m) is 30 per cent less than that of an M61 round, and the projectile drops a negligible distance – barely 10ft

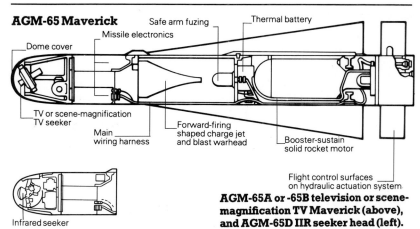

AGM-65 Maverick

Dome cover
TV or scene-magnification TV seeker
Missile electronics
Safe arm fuzing
Thermal battery
Main wiring harness
Forward-firing shaped charge jet and blast warhead
Booster-sustain solid rocket motor
Flight control surfaces on hydraulic actuation system

Infrared seeker

AGM-65A or -65B television or scene-magnification TV Maverick (above), and AGM-65D IIR seeker head (left).

Maverick launch zones

Feet in thousands

Mach 0.5
Mach 0.9
Mach 1.2

Feet in thousands: 10 20 30 40 50 60 70 80 90 100 110 120 130 140

Kilometres: 5 10 15 20 25 30 35 40

Nautical miles: 2 4 6 8 10 12 14 16 18 20 22

Above left: The Maverick's launch envelope varies with the speed and altitude of the launch aircraft, and with target range, though the Warthog pilot will be most concerned with the bottom left-hand corner.

Left: Preparing to load an AGM-65B scene-magnification Maverick onto an A-10 at Cairo West AB during a Bright Star exercise in 1981.

Below: After being loaded onto LAU-88 launchers, Mavericks are transferred to the special launcher rack, seen here at RAF Bentwaters, ready for mounting on the aircraft.

(3m) – in the process. The accuracy of the GAU-8/A, installed in the A-10, is rated at '5mil, 80 per cent', meaning that 80 per cent of rounds fired at 4,000ft (1,800m) will hit within a circle of 20ft (6.1m) radius; the M61 is rated at 8mil.

A very important innovation in the design of the GAU-8/A shells is the use of aluminium alloy cases in place of the traditional steel or brass. This alone adds 30 per cent to ammunition capacity for a given weight. The shells also have plastic driving bands to improve barrel life. They are imposing to examine and handle, measuring 11.4in (290mm) in length and weighing 1.53lb (694g) or more. There are four types in service. Two are common to most aircraft cannon: a practice round, and a general-purpose shell loaded with high-explosive/incendiary (HEI) compound. Specially developed for the A-10, however, are two armour-piercing incendiary (API) rounds. The USAF chose two companies, Aerojet and Honeywell, to develop and produce API shells for the A-10 under its 'second-source' philosophy: when items are acquired in large quantities, the USAF buys them from two organizations, and lets them bid competitively for each year's order.

The two API rounds are slightly different in detail, but basically are similar. Neither contains any explosive. Instead, they consist of a lightweight aluminium body, cast around a small 'penetrator' of smaller calibre than the shell. (The calibre is about 15mm.) It projects from the blunt body section, and the shell has a thin aluminium 'windscreen' to keep the shape aerodynamic. The penetrator is made of depleted uranium, a by-product of the enrichment process used to make nuclear fuel. The material has an extremely high density, comprising roughly two-thirds of the projectile's weight.

The result is that two-thirds of the total impact energy is concentrated in the small-calibre penetrator: enough energy to lift a thirty-ton weight one foot, delivered instantly to a penny-sized area. Not only is this ammunition capable of penetrating the top and side armour of an MBT, but the depleted uranium ignites on impact, sending a jet of flame into the vehicle.

Ammunition and feed system

The GAU-8/A ammunition is linkless, reducing weight and avoiding a great deal of potential for jamming. The feed system is double-ended: the spent cases are not ejected from the aircraft (which takes a great deal of force if the possibility of severe airframe damage is to be eliminated) but are cycled back into the ammunition drum. The feed system is based on that developed for later M61 installations, but uses more advanced design techniques and materials throughout, to save weight.

Inside the cylindrical outer drum is a rotating inner drum, resembling a huge, deeply cut worm gear. The helical channel which winds around this rotor holds the 1,350 shells; they are stored radially, with their tips toward the axis of the drum, and their bases are held in channels running the length of the fixed, outer drum. As the rotor turns, the shells are forced forward along the drum and into the complex of turning mechanisms and chutes leading to the gun.

Power for the gun and its feed mechanism is drawn from the A-10's dual hydraulic systems. Two hydraulic motors provide the total 77hp (57.4kW) needed to drive the system at its maximum firing rate. If either hydraulic system fails, the remaining motor can sustain the alternative 2,100rds/min rate.

Loading the linkless ammunition is the function of the only specialized piece of ground equipment used by the A-10. The Ammunition Loading System (ALS) resembles a trailer-mounted version of the GAU-8/A ammunition drum and feed system, and operates on the same principle, loading rounds and extracting empty cases simultaneously. A full load can be changed in less than 13 minutes.

GAU-8/A derivatives

Some of the GAU-8/A technology has been transferred into the smaller 25mm GAU-12/U Equalizer developed for the AV-8B, which is about the same size as the M61 but is considerably more lethal. GE has also developed the GAU-13, a four-barrel weapon using GAU-8A components, which has been tested in podded form, and the Avenger forms the basis for the Dutch-developed Goalkeeper naval air-defence gun. No current or contemplated aircraft other than the A-10, however, carries the full-up Avenger system. The weapon is simply too large. It measures 19ft 10.5in (5.06m) from the muzzle to the rearmost point of the ammunition feed system, and the ammunition drum alone is 34.5in (87.6cm) in diameter and 71.5in (181.6cm) long. With full ammunition, the system weighs 4,029lb (1,830kg).

In short, the GAU-8/A system, fully armed and ready to fire, is just about as long and as heavy as a Rolls-Royce or a full-size Cadillac. At its maximum firing rate, its average recoil force of 9,000lb (40kN) thrust is equal to the power of one of the A-10's engines. Operationally, the

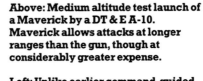

Above: Medium altitude test launch of a Maverick by a DT & E A-10. Maverick allows attacks at longer ranges than the gun, though at considerably greater expense.

Left: Unlike earlier command-guided air-to-surface missiles such as Bullpup, Maverick is a fire-and-forget weapon: the pilot designates the target as seen by the TV or infrared seeker head and displayed on his cockpit CRT, launches the missile and takes evasive action while it homes automatically on the selected target. This sequence shows the destruction of an M113 APC.

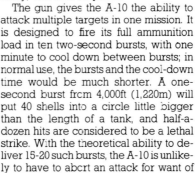

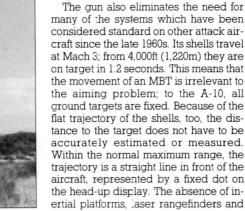

performance of the gun makes it as vital to the A-10's mission as the wings and engines. It has many unique attributes, and no other weapon, in service or under study, can take its place.

The gun gives the A-10 the ability to attack multiple targets in one mission. It is designed to fire its full ammunition load in ten two-second bursts, with one minute to cool down between bursts; in normal use, the bursts and the cool-down time would be much shorter. A one-second burst from 4,000ft (1,220m) will put 40 shells into a circle little bigger than the length of a tank, and half-a-dozen hits are considered to be a lethal strike. With the theoretical ability to deliver 15-20 such bursts, the A-10 is unlikely to have to abort an attack for want of firepower.

The gun also eliminates the need for many of the systems which have been considered standard on other attack aircraft since the late 1960s. Its shells travel at Mach 3; from 4,000ft (1,220m) they are on target in 1.2 seconds. This means that the movement of an MBT is irrelevant to the aiming problem; to the A-10, all ground targets are fixed. Because of the flat trajectory of the shells, too, the distance to the target does not have to be accurately estimated or measured. Within the normal maximum range, the trajectory is a straight line in front of the aircraft, represented by a fixed dot on the head-up display. The absence of inertial platforms, laser rangefinders and

other systems from the weapon-aiming loop not only simplifies the aircraft, but makes the pilot's workload less as well. Without the point-and-fire simplicity of the GAU-8/A, the A-10 concept of manoeuvring, medium-speed CAS with visual navigation and target acquisition would probably collapse due to excessive pilot workload.

The gun is extremely reliable. Stoppages are predicted to occur once in 150,000 rounds, or once in more than 100 missions when every round is fired. Even then, the weapon can often be cleared in flight by reversing the gun and feed mechanism and trying again. There is no guidance system to fail and nothing to be jammed or deceived. All this adds up to the fact that the kill probability of a GAU-8 burst is high: tests have shown that as many as half the bursts may be effective in a diving attack on the rear of a tank, and one third in side attacks.

AGM-65 Maverick

The gun is not only the primary weapon of the A-10, but it is one of only two weapons generally used by the aircraft. The other, the Hughes AGM-65 Maverick air-to-surface missile, complements the gun; it is also designed for attacks against hard, mobile precision targets, but from rather greater standoff distances. On the other hand, the Maverick does not give the A-10 the same sustained firing capability as the gun, and is not as fast-acting, and its cost per kill is very much greater. The cost of an early-model Maverick was quoted at $60,000 in 1981, versus $1,800 in ammunition and maintenance costs for a two-second burst from the cannon. The two systems, however, had a very similar kill probability (Pk) per pass, so the gun was far more economical.

Maverick was developed after the miserable failure of the command-guided Bullpup to accomplish anything in Vietnam. It was a very advanced concept for its day: a compact missile, designed for multiple carriage, which could guide itself autonomously to a precision target and destroy it with a large shaped-charge warhead. Its guidance system was based on television technol-

Alternative mission loads

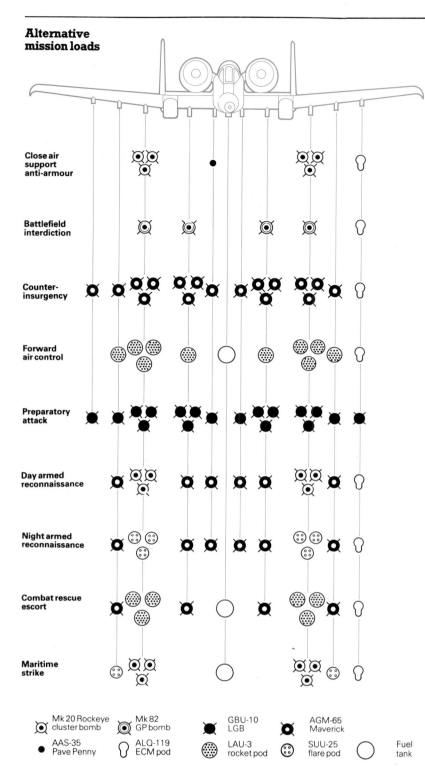

Close air support anti-armour						
Battlefield interdiction						
Counter-insurgency						
Forward air control						
Preparatory attack						
Day armed reconnaissance						
Night armed reconnaissance						
Combat rescue escort						
Maritime strike						

⊙ Mk 20 Rockeye cluster bomb	⊙ Mk 82 GP bomb	⬤ GBU-10 LGB	✦ AGM-65 Maverick	
● AAS-35 Pave Penny	⋒ ALQ-119 ECM pod	⊛ LAU-3 rocket pod	⊙ SUU-25 flare pod	◯ Fuel tank

Left: During operational evaluation, the USAF found the A-10 well-suited to the preparatory role, and unmatched as an escort; FAC capability was judged satisfactory, while other roles have been suggested by the makers.

Below: 333rd TFTS, 355th TTW A-10 en route to the Gila Bend range, with 25lb (11kg) BDU-33 practice bombs on wing-mounted triple and fuselage multiple ejection racks.

Right: A powered hoist is used to load a Mk 83 1,000lb (454kg) GP bomb under the wing of a 354th TFW A-10.

ogy. A stabilized video sensor provided a picture to a cockpit display, and fed a simple image-processing system in the missile. The pilot pointed the camera at the target using cockpit controls, commanded the seeker to lock on and launched the missile. The guidance system sensed relative movement by analyzing the video signal, and generated correction signals to keep the missile on target.

Two production versions of Maverick were built in the 1970s. The first was the basic AGM-65A, with an optical system designed to cover a 5deg cone in front of the aircraft – equivalent to the field of view of a 200mm lens on a 35mm camera. It was replaced in production by the AGM-65B, originally known as the Scene Magnification Maverick, which has a 2.5deg field of view, and is carried as a standard weapon by the A-10. Underwing pylons 3 and 9, immediately outboard of the landing gear pods, are each fitted to carry the LAU-88/A triple launcher for the AGM-65. Maverick is controlled from its own panel in the cockpit, consisting of a video screen and controls for slewing the seeker, switching from low to high magnification and locking the missile on to the target.

Maverick has proven to be successful and reliable, and 85 per cent of all missiles fired – including some fired in anger, in South-East Asia and the Middle East – are claimed to have hit their targets. More than 30,000 Mavericks have been built for the USAF and export customers. The weapon has only one serious drawback: it has to be fired from a point uncomfortably close to the target. The missile itself has a theoretical range of 6-7nm (11-13km) even under the most unfavourable conditions – launch from a slow aircraft, such as an A-10, at low level. However, its TV tracker will not normally lock on to a target outside 2-3nm (3.7-5.5km). This is because air is not perfectly transparent, and the attenuation of optical wavelengths with distance prevents the guidance circuitry from getting the clear, high-contrast image that it needs. Maverick takes 4-8 seconds to lock on, which is a long time in air combat, and particularly so when the launch sequence takes place within the envelope of standard air-defence systems such as the SA-8 Gecko. Multiple launches in a single attack pass are not practicable.

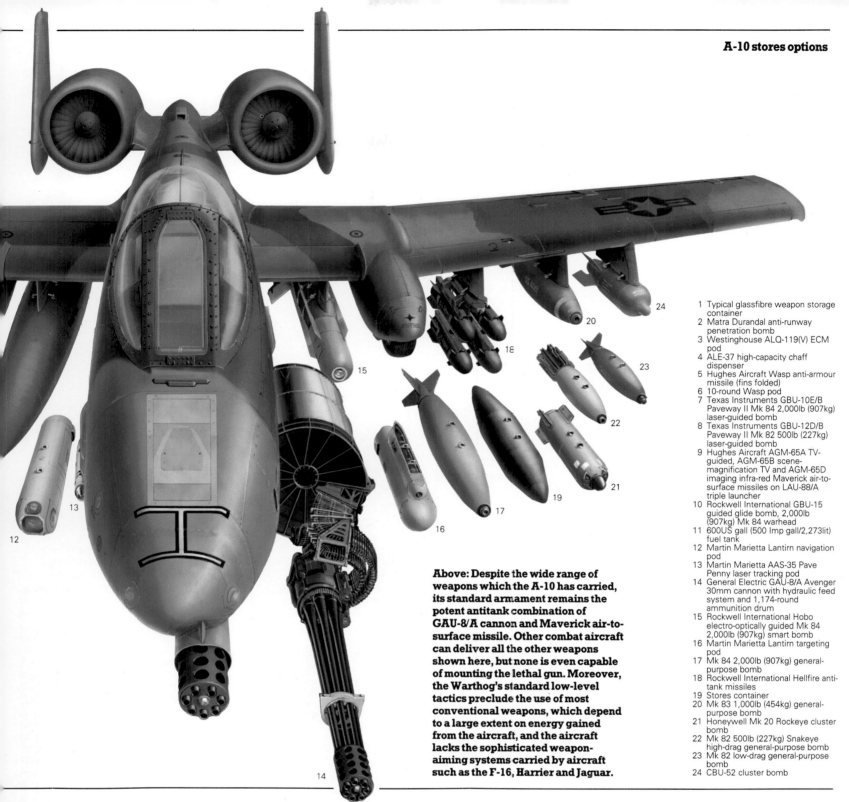

1 Typical glassfibre weapon storage container
2 Matra Durandal anti-runway penetration bomb
3 Westinghouse ALQ-119(V) ECM pod
4 ALE-37 high-capacity chaff dispenser
5 Hughes Aircraft Wasp anti-armour missile (fins folded)
6 10-round Wasp pod
7 Texas Instruments GBU-10E/B Paveway II Mk 84 2,000lb (907kg) laser-guided bomb
8 Texas Instruments GBU-12D/B Paveway II Mk 82 500lb (227kg) laser-guided bomb
9 Hughes Aircraft AGM-65A TV-guided, AGM-65B scene-magnification TV and AGM-65D imaging infra-red Maverick air-to-surface missiles on LAU-88/A triple launcher
10 Rockwell International GBU-15 guided glide bomb, 2,000lb (907kg) Mk 84 warhead
11 600US gall (500 Imp gall/2,273lit) fuel tank
12 Martin Marietta Lantirn navigation pod
13 Martin Marietta AAS-35 Pave Penny laser tracking pod
14 General Electric GAU-8/A Avenger 30mm cannon with hydraulic feed system and 1,174-round ammunition drum
15 Rockwell International Hobo electro-optically guided Mk 84 2,000lb (907kg) smart bomb
16 Martin Marietta Lantirn targeting pod
17 Mk 84 2,000lb (907kg) general-purpose bomb
18 Rockwell International Hellfire anti-tank missiles
19 Stores container
20 Mk 83 1,000lb (454kg) general-purpose bomb
21 Honeywell Mk 20 Rockeye cluster bomb
22 Mk 82 500lb (227kg) Snakeye high-drag general-purpose bomb
23 Mk 82 low-drag general-purpose bomb
24 CBU-52 cluster bomb

Above: Despite the wide range of weapons which the A-10 has carried, its standard armament remains the potent antitank combination of GAU-8/A cannon and Maverick air-to-surface missile. Other combat aircraft can deliver all the other weapons shown here, but none is even capable of mounting the lethal gun. Moreover, the Warthog's standard low-level tactics preclude the use of most conventional weapons, which depend to a large extent on energy gained from the aircraft, and the aircraft lacks the sophisticated weapon-aiming systems carried by aircraft such as the F-16, Harrier and Jaguar.

For this reason, the introduction of the AGM-65D infra-red (IR) Maverick was very significant for the A-10 force. IR video technology has been available for many years, but it has taken new advances in electronics to create missile-sized and missile-priced image-processing systems which will cull guidance data from IR images. Because IR wavelengths are relatively little affected by attenuation in 'clear air', the AGM-65D can lock on at twice the stand-off range possible with the AGM-65B. This is close to the maximum range of the SA-8, and brings multiple launches within the realms of practical possibility. These are being facilitated by the development of a rapid-fire modification for the LAU-88/A, incorporating a circuit which slews the seeker of the second missile on to the target area as the seeker of the first is locked-on.

The IR weapon is also less affected by dust and smoke on the battlefield, and the better-quality image allows the pilot to discriminate between different types of vehicle according to their characteristic IR 'signatures'. The weapon requires no mandatory modifications to any aircraft already fitted to fire the AGM-65B. However, it is equipped to receive targeting data from the aircraft's

weapon-aiming systems, and this capability can be used if the necessary control channel is installed.

The IR weapon's most important attribute is also of considerable value to the A-10. Since it operates identically by both day and night, the quality of the IR image presented to the pilot is basically the same. So, as expanded night-operating capability was sought, this characteristic was particularly useful, especially in the recent war in the Gulf when it assisted with location of targets

to be engaged by Maverick and other weapons in the Thunderbolt's arsenal.

Photographs of the A-10 loaded from wingtip to wingtip with weapons have helped to spread the impression that the aircraft was designed as an ordnance truck, primarily intended to carry a massive external load. This is not exactly true. The A-10 can lift a large warload because it was designed to use short fields, manoeuvre and fight while carrying a more moderate load. If the manoeuvring requirements are less severe,

and a longer runway is available, the aircraft can lift a larger load. For an antitank mission from a forward operating base, however, six Mavericks and ammunition for the GAU-8/A constitute a full offensive load. Between them, the missiles and the gun are well suited to the A-10's primary mission, like most other aspects of the design.

In service with the USAF, the A-10 has been cleared to drop and fire a wide variety of weapons. These include the straightforward Mk 82 '500lb' bomb (which actually weighs 565lb/256kg); the A-10 can carry 28 such weapons. For use against troops or soft-skinned vehicles, the A-10 can carry cluster weapons such as Rockeye, CBU-52/58/71 and the British BL755. More sophisticated weapons include the GBU-12 laser-guided glide bomb, based on the 3,000lb Mk 84.

The A-10, however, is not particularly suited to deliver many of these weapons

Left: Bomb-carrying trials with the first DT & E A-10. Maximum load is 16,000lb, distributed between 11 pylons, though the extreme outboard wing pylons, limited to 1,000lb (454kg), are rarely used for anything but an ALQ-119 ECM pod.

Standard and INS HUD symbology and control units

The A-10 was designed for visual navigation and target acquisition, and the original avionics suite was as simple as possible, the head-up display using only the basic symbology shown below. The switch to low-level tactics, especially in poor visibility, made an inertial navigation system necessary, resulting in the expanded symbology shown right.

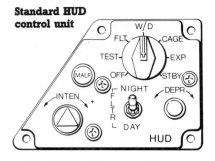

Standard HUD labels:
Fixed target alignment cross · Gun inhibit · Roll test target · Aiming reticle · Roll bar · Airspeed · Altitude · Pipper · Reticle depression · Pitch angle · LSS reticle · LSS direction line

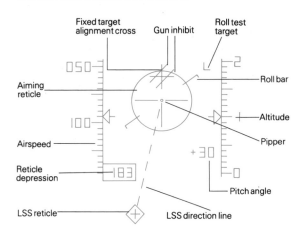

INS HUD labels:
Total velocity vector · Destination index (tadpole) · Gun cross · Reticle eyebrows · Distance to go · Time to go · Altitude tape · Aiming reticle · Vertical velocity indicator · Airspeed tape · Pipper · TISL diamond and line · Pipper target · TISL target · Flight path/pitch angle · Depression numeric · Steer point · Flight path ladder · Heading scale

Standard HUD control unit

INS HUD control unit

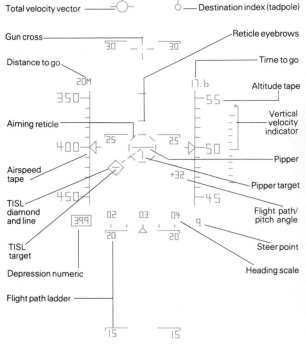

Above: The head-up display unit developed by Kaiser Electronics specially for the A-10 has been improved to incorporate inputs from the inertial navigation system.

---

in the face of intense defences. As noted earlier, it does not possess many of the features which are standard on other light strike types, such as the F-16, Harrier and Jaguar. All these aircraft have some sort of weapon-aiming system which can measure the velocity of the aircraft relative to the ground and the distance to the target, compute the trajectory of whatever ordnance may be on board and indicate the precise moment to release the weapon. The A-10 has no means of measuring ground velocity, such as a high-accuracy inertial platform; it has no means of measuring range to the target and no weapons-release computer. Accurate attack with any weapon other than Maverick and the GAU-8/A is possible only in a steep, low-airspeed dive from medium altitude, a somewhat foolhardy tactic in the presence of SAMs or AAA.

It is not that the A-10 is deficient in its relative inability to use such weapons safely and effectively; just that it is a specialized aircraft, and is used as such. In the GAU-8/A and Maverick, it carries two proven and reliable precision-attack weapons which operate without complex aiming systems. The aircraft can dispense with them, and is thereby made more reliable and less costly.

Avionic systems

The original concept of the A-10 was for an aircraft that would be as devoid of avionics as the original Skyraider: no inertial navigation system, no complex displays, and no automatic flight control system or other pilot aids. It would be equipped with communications equipment, simple beacon-type navigation gear, and a straightforward head-up display with limited weapon-aiming symbology. While the A-10 is still closer to the Skyraider than any other aircraft in the USAF

inventory, contact with reality has, as usual, changed plans to some extent.

The changing threat and the changing tactics needed to meet it have been the main motivations behind additions to the A-10's equipment list. More mobile missile systems, and the need to fly the entire mission at low altitude, are among them. The basic system has been little changed, though. The instrument panel facing the pilot is simple, with standard flight instruments and dual sets of gauges for the TF34 engines. To the pilot's right is the video display for the Maverick missile. The primary flight instrument is the Kaiser Electronics head-up display. This is a specially developed, uncomplicated unit which displays aircraft pitch and roll attitude, airspeed and altitude. Weapon-aiming systems on the initial production aircraft amounted to a fixed gunsight reticle on the HUD and the Maverick control panel.

The only addition to the weapon-aiming system to date is the Martin Marietta AAS-35 Pave Penny laser target-identification set, introduced to squadron use in early 1978. Pave Penny

Above: The cockpit reflects the absence of sophisticated avionics, with standard flight instruments and the Maverick TV display to the right.

acts as a link between the attack aircraft and a forward air controller (FAC), who may be in a ground vehicle, a helicopter or an OV-10 reconnaissance aircraft. It is a low-cost, compact and lightweight device, 32in (81cm) long and weighing 32lb (14.5kg), which scans the area ahead of the aircraft for laser radiation. The FAC designates a target with his own laser equipment, Pave Penny picks up the reflection of the coded beam, and places a HUD symbol over the target. The A-10 pilot then takes over and attacks in the usual way. Pave Penny is carried on an unusual pylon mounting, attached to the starboard side of the forward fuselage; the usual nose installation is ruled out by the proximity of the gun muzzle with its associated shockwaves and vibration.

Defensive avionics on the first A-10s were confined to the Itek ALR-46 radar-warning receiver (RWR) system, a fairly simple piece of equipment with anten-

nae built into the nose and tail of the aircraft. This has since been upgraded to the improved ALR-64 and ALR-69 models, to cope with the changing frequencies of Soviet air-defence radars. All the systems feed a simple plan-position indicator (PPI) scope in the cockpit, and show the bearing and approximate range of threatening radars. The system is most useful against the Shilka air-defence gun; the RWR shows the Shilka's position before the A-10 gets within range of its quad-barrelled 23mm cannon.

ECM protection

For active ECM protection in a high-threat environment, the A-10 normally carries a single Westinghouse ALQ-119 electronic countermeasures (ECM) pod on the outermost starboard pylon. The ALQ-119 has been superseded by the same company's ALQ-131 on later USAF aircraft such as the F-16. This is not to say that the older pod is ineffective or obsolete, but the newer system is effective against a wider range of threats, and can jam a greater number of frequencies.

The A-10 does, however, carry a very comprehensive internal decoy system, in the shape of the Tracor ALE-40. Built into formerly empty space in the landing gear pods and wingtips, the ALE-40 consists of 16 batteries of small tubes – 30 tubes to a battery – housing a total of 480 pyrotechnically-fired decoys. Some of these are flares, designed to lead an infra-red homing missile away from the A-10; the rest contain chaff, or thin strips of aluminium foil, and deploy into a loose cloud of metal after being ejected from the aircraft. Chaff is the oldest form of ECM, and under certain circumstances is still one of the most effective deception techniques and one of the hardest to counter. Decoys are a last-ditch defence

Typical head-up displays

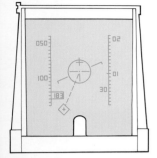

Test mode

Cage mode

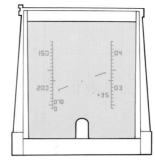

Flight mode

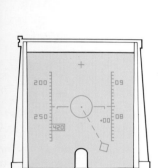

Expanded mode

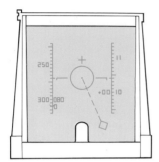

Weapon delivery mode

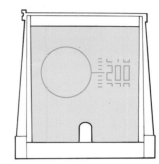

Standby mode

against missile attack; the pilot fires his decoys and simultaneously pulls a hard break, hoping that the missile's tendency to assume that the aircraft will continue in a straight path will lead it to follow the decoys rather than the real target.

Essentially, the USAF considers that tactics are more important than ECM to the close-support mission. This is why the A-10's equipment is relatively unsophisticated, and why the aircraft is not scheduled to receive the ALQ-165 advanced self-protection jammer (ASPJ), when it becomes available later in the 1980s. ECM is most necessary when an aircraft is exposed for long periods of time to the larger and more sophisticated missile systems: A-10 tactics are geared to avoiding such systems. Also, the A-10 is intended to carry the attack to close quarters, where large and complex systems are close to their minimum range and increasingly cumbersome. In brief, the A-10 is designed and used to need less help from sophisticated ECM than an F-16 or F-15.

Flight control and navigation

The A-10 has no automatic flight control system (AFCS), but is fitted with a stability augmentation system (SAS). The primary function of the SAS is to improve the stability of the aircraft as a weapons platform, and to make the aircraft respond more consistently to the controls; it is a simple, single-channel system and has been upgraded since the aircraft entered service. The SAS also provides warning of an excessive angle of attack, and impending stall, via a stick-shaker.

In one major respect, it was soon discovered, the philosophy of austerity had been taken too far: the A-10's lack of a built-in, autonomous navigation system. Like many features of the aircraft, this went back to the original A-X concept, and to US tactics of the late 1960s. The A-10 was expected to cruise to its loitering point at low-to-medium altitude, where the pilot would not have to follow terrain and Tacan beacons would provide necessary navigational data. But at low level Tacan is of limited use because its line-of-sight transmissions are usually blocked by terrain or the curvature of the earth. A-10 pilots in Europe found themselves navigating with 1/50,000-scale maps across their knees, while

trying to avoid both the defences and the ground.

The solution was to add an inertial navigation system (INS) to the A-10. While some critics charged that installing INS ran counter to the basic philosophy of the A-10, there was nothing else to be done: in sustained low-level flight, the need to map-read pushed the pilot's workload to unacceptably high levels, while the need to pull up periodically to search for landmarks compromised the security of the formation.

A standard USAF INS, the ASN-141, was incorporated in the last 283 A-10s, starting in 1980, and the INS-equipped aircraft were first delivered to Europe, where the need was greatest. As production of new A-10s ran down, modification kits were produced for earlier aircraft; a contract covering the last batch of these was announced in April

1984, and the entire fleet was to be upgraded by mid-1987.

In the original A-10, the HUD gave the pilot basic flight information – speed, altitude and aircraft pitch and roll angle. The new system adds a wealth of data: vertical speed and flightpath (the angle at which the aircraft is climbing or diving), actual heading, the direction to steer to a pre-programmed waypoint or target location, and the distance and time to go to the next waypoint. Essentially, it relieves the pilot of the need to map-read and fly evasively at the same time. Navigation inputs can be made when convenient, and appear as clear directions on the HUD. The new equipment calls for little change to the cockpit; the HUD control unit is modified to control the new functions and an INS panel is added.

Because INS data would be projected on to the head-up display, Kaiser was made responsible for devising the INS installation. The chosen solution was to improve the HUD, and link it to the existing central air-data computer and the INS through a digital data-handling system or 'bus'. The existing HUD projection system is retained, but a completely new symbol generator of much greater power is installed. It is still fed with data from the conventional heading, attitude and reference system, but this pitch and roll information is used for back-up purposes only. The most important data is fed to the HUD through dual digital buses, designed to the USAF's MIL-STD-1553B standard.

Another improvement accompanies the introduction of INS. The A-10 was originally fitted with a conventional pressure altimeter, providing readings above sea level, but this was soon found to be inadequate on prolonged low-level flights over Europe's rolling hills. A standard APN-194 radar altimeter has re-

Pave Penny attack scenario

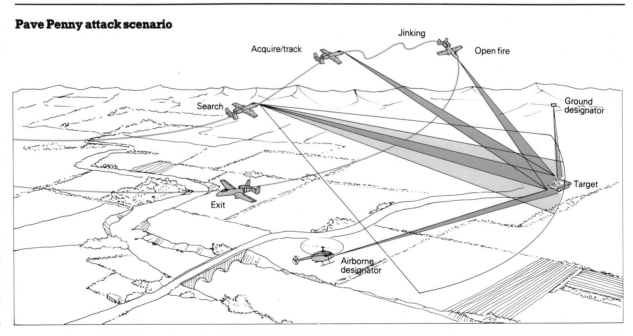

Above: the AAS-38 Pave Penny laser seeker pod allows the A-10 to acquire targets designated by forward air controllers, who may be airborne or with the troops on the ground. The pod detects the reflected radiation from the target and indicates it on the HUD, and the pilot then manoeuvres into position for a standard gun or Maverick attack.

Right: External avionics pods on a 354th TFW A-10 at Myrtle Beach AFB. The Pave Penny is offset from the usual nose position to avoid the gun blast; the ALQ-119 jamming pod is normally carried on the outboard starboard wing pylon.

placed it on late-production and retrofitted A-10s.

Lantirn

The digital databus system may also provide the basis for a vast step forward in the A-10's operational capability: the introduction of the Lantirn (low-altitude navigation, and targeting by infra-red at night) night-attack system in the late 1980s. Lantirn, being developed by the USAF and Martin Marietta with the help of a team of major subcontractors, is an ambitious programme aimed at creating a single affordable, easily installed package which will give any of TAC's aircraft the ability to penetrate at low level, and find and strike precision targets, at night.

Lantirn has drawn some fire from critics, and its future is not completely assured. However, it is now an integral part of the very important F-15E dual-role fighter programme, and there is definitely increasing concern over the ability of Soviet armoured units to operate effectively at night. At present, only a few specialized TAC aircraft can operate outside daylight hours, and they are certainly too few in number to make much of an impact against a large-scale armoured assault. Lantirn is planned to make 700 more TAC aircraft capable of flying in terrain and weather cover at night, and carrying out precision attacks in clear air at night.

The Lantirn system consists of a set of highly miniaturized sensors and image-processing equipment, mounted in two external pods and feeding data via 1553B

databuses to an advanced HUD. One pod handles navigation, and the other handles targeting. The navigation pod houses an advanced terrain-following radar (TFR) developed by Texas Instruments, together with a wide-angle forward-looking infra-red (Flir) system.

On a clear night, the pilot will fly at low level using a Flir image, superimposed on the real world by means of the HUD. The latter is planned to be a Marconi Avionics design, using holographic techniques; these are based on the diffraction of light, rather than reflection. A holographic HUD screen can be almost perfectly transparent to most light wavelengths, and be an almost perfect reflector of the wavelength chosen for HUD imagery. It is therefore possible to superimpose a detailed Flir image without obliterating the real world. It also differs from the normal HUD in that it can include the wide-angle picture needed for low-level navigation.

The Flir is useless, however, in cloud or rain. The TFR is needed to penetrate low cloud en route to the target and to let down through the weather when the cloudbase is low or unknown. It takes advantage of new processing techniques to allow higher rates of turn under

Lantirn targeting pod

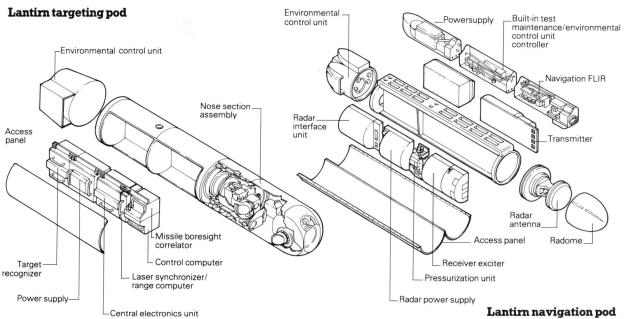

Lantirn navigation pod

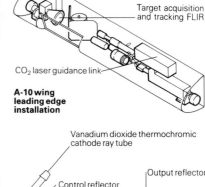

Hypervelocity missile pod installation

CO₂laser guidance link

Target acquisition and tracking FLIR

Fire control installation

Target acquisition and tracking FLIR

CO₂ laser guidance link

A-10 wing leading edge installation

Vanadium dioxide thermochromic cathode ray tube

Output reflector

Control reflector

Laser medium

Deflected beam output

Electronically scanned laser radar sensor

Above: Test launch of a prototype LTV Aerospace hypervelocity missile at White Sands Missile Range, where the missile demonstrated its ability to receive guidance commands from the carbon dioxide laser despite the smoke plume.

Right: Model of an A-10 with two hypervelocity missile (HVM) pods.

Right and above right: The components of the HVM system, which could provide a logical extension of the A-10's standard armoury: the high speed of the rocket will minimize exposure to defensive systems, and the single laser scanner can direct several missiles at once.

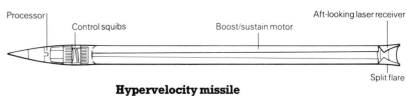

Processor

Control squibs

Boost/sustain motor

Aft-looking laser receiver

Split flare

Hypervelocity missile

TFR control than was possible with earlier systems, and, in straight flight, to provide the maximum possible cover with the least possible transmission power and time, reducing the possibility of detection by hostile EW systems. The advanced HUD can display Flir imagery and TFR data simultaneously.

The targeting pod contains a narrow-angle Flir, feeding a 'telephoto' image to a head-down display in the cockpit, and a laser system which can act either as a rangefinder or a designator for laser-guided weapons. Spotting a target in the Flir image on the HUD, the pilot can bring the targeting pod's Flir to bear, and identify the target. He then has a number of options. Probably the most potent weapon for use with Lantirn is the IR Maverick. As noted earlier, the missile's seeker can be 'cued' on to the target by the aircraft systems, so the lock-on would be automatic and immediate. The pilot need only check that the missile has locked on, fire it and slew the targeting Flir to the next objective. Alternatively, he can use the laser system, either designating a target for a laser-guided bomb, or obtaining accurate range information for the release of a free-fall iron or cluster bomb.

Lantirn was launched into accelerated development in the late 1970s, but in September 1981 the pace of the programme was slowed down sharply, so as not to start production before the system had been thoroughly developed and tested. One of its more advanced features, an automatic target recogniser (ATR) intended to discriminate between MBTs, mobile SAMs and other armoured

vehicles, was judged in 1983 to be too ambitious for near-term development, and has been 'uncoupled' from the rest of the programme; development of the elements outlined above was reported at that time to be proceeding according to plan. In mid-1984, prototype testing of the complete Lantirn system was under way aboard an F-16B at Edwards AFB, and this was due to continue until the end of the year. The current schedule calls for delivery of the first production Lantirn system in July 1987.

Of the 700 Lantirn pods to be acquired by the USAF by 1993, it is not clear how many may be allotted to the A-10. The larger navigation pod will be carried on the starboard fuselage pylon, and the targeting pod will be slung beneath the port inboard wing. However, it is probably fair to say that the F-15E will enjoy top priority for Lantirn, followed by the F-16 and A-16. The A-10 will be bringing up the rear. In any event, the balance of the A-10 force will remain daytime-only aircraft in the foreseeable future.

Another improvement under consideration for the A-10 force is a ground proximity warning system (GPWS), similar in principle to the computerized alert system now fitted to most Western airliners and developed by Sundstrand, a world leader in GPWS. TAC issued the requirement after reviewing the A-10 accident record and discovering that a number of mishaps were due to high pilot workload or 'task saturation' – the latter being defined as concentrating on one task for more than five seconds. Scanning for targets, seeking firing opportunities and evading defences at

low level, some pilots had simply flown into trees or the terrain.

A prototype GPWS was under test on an A-10 in early 1984. Like a civil GPWS, the system integrates airspeed, attitude and radar altimeter data and provides an electronically synthesized voice warning; however, the warning 'modes', or the envelopes within which the system will command or advise the pilot, are different. In low-level flight, the system will warn if the aircraft is below a preset altitude, and will also issue a 'roll out' command if the aircraft is low and the bank angle exceeds 45deg. The GPWS will also warn the pilot if the aircraft is too close to rising terrain – taking into account speed, the slope of the ground and the performance of the aircraft – and will order the pilot to abort an attack if he is in danger of hitting the ground.

Hypervelocity missile

Another proposed change for the A-10, not yet part of official planning, is its use as the first carrier for a new type of weapon, the hypervelocity missile (HVM) under development by Vought. As its name suggests, the HVM flies at extremely high speeds: almost 3,000kt (5,500km/h) or Mach 4.5. Because of this high speed, and the missile's accordingly short flight time, the launch aircraft can track the missile to impact without becoming vulnerable to defensive systems; costly, bulky fire-and-forget guidance systems are therefore unnecessary. The missile hits the target so fast – 50 per cent faster than the muzzle velocity of the GAU-8 – that the warhead can be eliminated as well, because a bundle of

depleted-uranium or tungsten rods will destroy any conceivable armour.

The guidance system tested by Vought in 1983 consisted of a laser beam scanning a raster pattern (like the electron gun in the TV tube). The missile's electronics sense its position in the raster, and steer it towards the centre; control of the projectile is carried out by firing small explosive squibs through ports in its side. However, the missile itself is spin-stabilised and automatically guided to maintain its trajectory. Its speed renders target movement relatively insignificant, so it needs no more than the occasional mid-course update on the way to its target. Because of this feature, the single laser scanner can direct several missiles simultaneously on to different targets.

Vought estimates that a tank-killing HVM weighing less than 80lb (36.3kg) would have a range of 3 miles (4.8km), several times that of the GAU-8/A. On the A-10, an HVM system would use Lantirn or a similar device for targeting, and the HVM guidance system could be built into the wing leading edge. Two underwing pods would each accommodate 19 HVMs. With its explosive control system, the HVM has no moving parts, and the cost of each round was estimated at $5,000 in 1981. The missile and guidance system were demonstrated in 1983, and Vought has proposed a two-year prototype programme leading to live firings from an A-10. By April 1984, however, funding for such an effort had not been obtained. But it would be a suitable first for the A-10, sustaining its position as the most lethally armed of all tactical aircraft.

Deployment

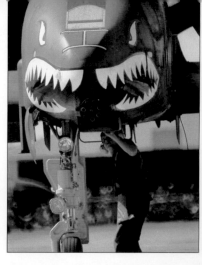

Almost every tactical command in the US Air Force has an A-10 unit on strength, and Reserve and Air National Guard units also use the A-10. However, the USAF bought no more A-10s than it had originally planned, and acquired only the basic single-seat A-10A version. Fairchild's efforts to sell a two-seat night-capable version to the USAF went unrewarded, and neither did the type find export customers, who preferred the more glamorous supersonic fighters. The last A-10 was delivered to the USAF early in 1984.

As a rule, unless things go badly wrong, the USAF buys more of every type of aircraft than it originally planned. As the end of planned production approaches a number of factors conspire to keep the line open. The aircraft is cheap to buy, compared with new types: newer aircraft are seldom ready as soon as had been envisaged, and there may be gaps in the front line to fill. New versions of the type may have been developed to carry out different missions, expanding the service's requirement.

At the same time, US combat aircraft nearly always find export markets. While US aircraft manufacturers often bewail the advantageous terms offered by foreign competitors in the commercial aircraft market, they are less vocal about the excellent credit facilities provided to their military customers through the Pentagon's FMS (foreign military sales) organization.

The A-10 has been an exception. Production ceased in 1984 after the exact quantity planned had been delivered. The last aircraft off the line was the same subtype as the first – in this respect, the A-10 was unique among US combat aircraft. Nor have any A-10s been sold for export. A disappointing outcome for Fairchild, this has been no fault of the

aircraft or those who developed it; the programme has been trouble-free, and what cost overruns did occur were due to outside circumstances such as production-rate cutbacks and inflation. The aircraft does exactly what it was designed to do, and does it well.

The A-10's real problem came from outside the programme; it was fast, it was manoeuvrable, it was everything that a fighter should be, and it was called the F-16. It did not even exist, except as General Dynamics' Model 401 design study, when the USAF ordered the YA-10A prototypes, and it was a year away from its first flight when the A-10 was selected for production. At that time, in early 1973, the YF-16/YF-17 fly-off was not expected to lead to a production programme. Within just over a year, the two types were competing for a massive USAF order. The change had come about under pressure from Secretary of Defense James Schlesinger, and was motivated by two factors: concern over the cost of replacing all the USAF's fighters with the costly and sophisticated F-15, and the prospect of securing a massive order from Europe. The latter could, and did, assure US dominance of the international fighter scene for a decade or more.

The F-16 emerged victorious in the fly-off, and won the European order. It was not intended as a substitute for the A-10, but as a running-mate for the F-15; however, the simple laws of manufacturing economics put the GD and Fairchild aircraft in a kind of competition. Like any manufactured object, aircraft are cheaper if built in the largest possible quantities. Moreover, the graph of unit cost versus production rate is not a straight line, but a curve, and the price for each aircraft increases very rapidly at low rates. In the second half of the 1970s the USAF was in the middle of a post-Vietnam budgetary squeeze. There was simply not enough money available to buy three types of fighter – F-15s, F-16s and A-10s – at economical production rates. If the USAF continued indefinitely to buy all three types at the low rates it could afford, it would get far fewer aircraft at much higher prices.

Losing to the F-16

The F-15 was sacrosanct. The Air Force wanted as many F-15s as possible from every year's budget. Between the A-10 and the F-16 there was very little room for choice. Four NATO allies were committed to the F-16, and if the USAF was to stop after buying, say,

650 aircraft, they would be faced with a massive price increase for any future batches of F-16s. The Europeans were relying on USAF partnership in upgrading and improving the aircraft. Neither should it be forgotten that TAC, more than any other air command in the world, is a fighter pilot's service, and as a result has a built-in aversion to an aircraft that cannot chase MiGs.

The F-16 was also a dual-role fighter/strike aircraft, a concept which had been poison when the A-10/F-15 requirements were drafted, but which was now returning to favour thanks to economic pressure and new technology. Improved radar, better HUDs and accurate INS were making it possible for a relatively simple fighter to deliver ordnance with acceptable accuracy. There was no clear point at which the USAF decided to stop the A-10 programme; all purchases are negotiated independently, year by year. By the late 1970s, however, it was

Above: An 81st TFW A-10 ready for collection alongside a Virginia ANG F-105. The pilots of the 81st collected new Warthogs as their old ones fell due for maintenance.

Below: An 81st TFW pilot prepares for a mission during a Reforger '82 exercise. Despite the addition of an inertial system, maps are still important for visual navigation.

Left: Although based in England, the 81st regularly deploys to Germany for training: one of the wing's aircraft waits for takeoff clearance at a dispersal point during Reforger '82.

becoming increasingly clear that the USAF would stop production of the A-10 after buying the 700+ aircraft which had been set as the necessary force level to handle a strictly defined CAS mission. All other air-to-ground tasks would be handled by the dual-purpose F-16.

The A-10's technical and operational success helped to bring production to a close. This sounds paradoxical, but consider the cumulative impact of the following facts. At any time, the USAF's frontline A-10s have a mission-capable rate around 75 per cent – that is to say, three-quarters of the aircraft in the squadrons are fit to fly under wartime conditions. Despite being used almost exclusively in low-altitude, visual close-support missions, the A-10 has one of the lowest accident rates of any USAF fighter in history. It can be turned round between missions faster than any other USAF aircraft, and it can sustain operations from dispersed locations close to the front; for these reasons, it can sustain the kind of sortie rates which other aircraft only reach in an all-out surge. Lastly, its toughness, simplicity and ease of repair give the operating units a unique capability to 're-generate' after taking hits in action. Unfortunately for Fairchild, the foregoing adds up to one conclusion: a few A-10s go a long way.

Deliveries of the A-10 to operational units began in March 1977, a few months after the first aircraft had reached the designated training wing. As is normal practice, a unit based in the continental USA (CONUS) was assigned the first aircraft: the 354th Tactical Fighter Wing (TFW) at Myrtle Beach AFB, South Carolina. One reason for the choice of base was its proximity to a large gunnery test and training range. The first of its squadrons to be declared fully operational was the 356th Tactical Fighter Squadron (TFS), in October 1977.

Deployment proceeded steadily rather than rapidly, because the production decision had been delayed until flight tests were well advanced, and Congress had repeatedly reduced the number of A-10s to be bought each year. By mid-1977 the USAF still had only 55 A-10s, divided among the 354th TFW at Myrtle Beach, the designated training organisation – the 355th Tactical Fighter Training Wing (TFTW) at Davis-Monthan AFB, Arizona – and the 57th Tactical Training Wing at Nellis AFB, which was tasked with developing A-10 tactics.

From 1977, however, USAF priority was to field the A-10 in Europe. In August

six A-10s of the 355th TFTW flew to Sembach, West Germany, to participate in the Autumn Forge series of exercises. Together with the JAWS tests carried out in late 1977, this experimental deployment provided a great deal of information on the best way to use the A-10 against typical Warsaw pact targets in European weather.

81st TFW

In February 1978, the USAF announced that the 81st TFW, based at RAF Bentwaters and also operating from nearby Woodbridge, would receive the A-10 as a replacement for the F-4D Phantom. Instead of deploying two wings, as had been planned, the 81st would be expanded into a 'superwing', with six 18-aircraft flying squadrons instead of the usual three. From early 1978, the main thrust of USAF A-10 activity was to get the 81st operational as soon as possible. The 355th TFTW played a key role in the programme, using experience gained in European tests and JAWS trials, processing pilots through the training system at Davis-Monthan.

Pilots for the 81st TFW were drawn from four groups, in roughly equal amounts: new graduates fresh from Air Training Command; T-38 instructor pilots, ready for assignment to their first operational wing; the 81st's own F-4D pilots, with experience of European operating conditions; and pilots returning to flight status from other assignments. This philosophy worked well: the F-4 pilots and the last-mentioned group included a good deal of combat support and FAC experience, but the unit was not so top-heavy with experience that younger pilots would be denied any chance of developing their own leadership skills.

Milestones in the transition programme included the delivery of three A-10As to Bentwaters for 'hands-on' maintenance training on August 24, 1978 and four more examples followed in early December. A huge step towards regaining fully operational status occurred on January 25, 1979 when the 92nd TFS ferried a batch of 18 Thunderbolts to Bentwaters. Indeed, this outfit was actually considered mission-ready at the moment of arrival and rapid progress ensued, with four squadrons in place by the end of 1979 and two of the forward operating locations (FOLs) already activated, at Sembach and Ahlhorn in West Germany. Two more FOLs – at Leipheim and Norvenich – attained operational status in 1980, each usually having a complement of around eight aircraft, and the last two squadrons had also arrived in England by the summer of that year.

The 81st continued to be the priority A-10 unit and the initial batch of Thunderbolts were not destined to remain in Europe for too long, being replaced by factory-fresh machines embodying the latest equipment as they rolled from the assembly line at Hagerstown. In this way, the 81st was the first unit to have INS and other important features on its entire fleet.

Bentwaters and Woodbridge still support A-10 operations at the present time but a fairly significant reduction in the size of the 81st's inventory occurred during 1987 when two of the Bentwaters-based squadrons (the 509th and 511th TFSs) were reassigned to the 10th TFW at Alconbury. Moving in the reverse direction was Alconbury's long-resident 'aggressor' squadron which was henceforth to fly F-16C Fighting Falcons from Bentwaters. This change-over was accomplished in the spring and summer, with the 509th TFS being formally reallocated to the 10th TFW on April 15 and the 511th TFS duly followed suit on July 1. Along with a complement of about 36 aircraft, the 10th TFW also picked-up responsibility for the FOL at Ahlhorn, this revised arrangement leaving the 81st with four squadrons (the 78th and 91st at Woodbridge plus the 92nd and 510th at Bentwaters) as well as management of the FOLs at Sembach, Leipheim and Norvenich.

Disposition has remained unaltered since then, but big changes are in the offing, with both Bentwaters and Woodbridge due to close during the early 1990s and their A-10s will no doubt be ferried back to the USA as part of the run-down of European-based forces. As to the Alconbury unit, this too is to stand-down as an A-10 outfit, with one of the two squadrons scheduled to return to the USA in late 1991, but it appears that about two dozen aircraft will be retained in Europe as part of a composite Wing to be established at Spangdahlem, Germany.

This will allow USAFE to keep a token 'tank-busting' force in place although it is conceivable that the Warthog mission may become primarily forward air control orientated, using aircraft designated as OA-10As. Leaving aside such considerations, USAFE can of course be hastily reinforced by units from the USA should the need arise.

Responsibility for that reinforcement would primarily be entrusted to Tactical Air Command which currently numbers three combat-ready Warthog Wings in its line-up, as well as the Arizona-based training establishment. One of these is the 354th TFW at Myrtle Beach, which was the first operational unit to receive the type. Another is the 23rd TFW at England AFB, Louisiana which converted from the A-7D Corsair II at the start of the 1980s. In accordance with TAC's philosophy of mobility, both of these Wings do regularly make short deployments to overseas bases, most notably in Europe.

Finally, there is the 602nd TACW (Tactical Air Control Wing) at Davis-Monthan. Specializing in forward air control duties, one squadron assigned to this wing (the 23rd TASS – Tactical Air Support Squadron) began receiving the OA-10A as a replacement for the OA-37B in October 1987. This now operates about two dozen aircraft, some of which were committed to combat action during the war with Iraq, alongside pure attack-dedicated A-10As drawn from AFRES, TAC and USAFE.

Two other overseas-based units operate the A-10, both now falling within the Pacific Air Forces (PacAF) sphere of influence, although it wasn't always thus. At Eielson AFB, Alaska, the 343rd TFW directs the activities of a single squadron (the 18th TFS) with a mix of A-10As and OA-10As for battlefield air interdiction (BAI) and forward air control (FAC)

Right: The shark's mouth nose markings made famous by the American Volunteer Group in China were adopted by the 23rd TFG that replaced it, and are still used by the 23rd TFW, one of only two A-10 combat wings based in the continental United States. The 23rd and 354th TFWs, along with the rest of TAC's combat wings, constitute the USAF's ready reserve element.

Above: The 118th TFS, 103rd TFG, Connecticut ANG, based at Bradley Field, is one of five Air National Guard squadrons equipped with the A-10.

Right: The USAF's other part-time volunteer element, the Air Force Reserve, has one training and four regular A-10 squadrons: the distinctive Warthog nose marking is the trademark of the 917th TFW.

tasks. Until the summer of 1990, this unit formed part of the Alaskan Air Command but that agency was eliminated in a high-level reorganisation and it now reports to the Eleventh Air Force, which in turn constitutes part of PacAF.

PacAF operation of the A-10 actually dates back to the early 1980s when a single squadron (the 25th TFS) was established at Suwon, South Korea, as part of the 51st TFW and this remained in being until shortly before the end of the decade when it was eliminated. Deactivation did not, however, mean the disappearance of the A-10, for most of the examples previously assigned to the 25th TFS now formed the complement of the 19th TASS as OA-10As. Subordinate to the 5th TACG (Tactical Air Support Group), it is primarily concerned with forward air control duties.

AFRES and ANG
The balance of the A-10 force in CONUS is assigned to the US Air Force Reserve (AFRES) and the Air National Guard (ANG). With its moderate maintenance requirements, the A-10 was a logical choice for these forces and quite a few examples of the Warthog were delivered direct from the factory to these second-line echelons.

AFRES units have remained virtually unchanged throughout the past decade and presently number five squadrons. Single squadrons reside at Richards-Gebaur, Missouri; Grissom, Indiana and New Orleans, Louisiana while Barksdale, Louisiana has two squadrons one of which is concerned solely with training pilots.

ANG units also number five, but these are more widespread. Four are concerned solely with BAI, flying from locations in the states of Connecticut, Maryland, Massachusetts and Wisconsin but it should be noted that a fifth unit in New York converted from the A-10A to the F-16A Fighting Falcon between November 1988 and May 1989. Thunderbolt IIs made surplus by this re-equipment were redesignated as OA-10As and used to replace the OA-37B Dragonfly with a FAC-dedicated ANG outfit in Pennsylvania.

Apart from key executive positions, AFRES and ANG flying units are both manned by part-time volunteers and operate in a similar way, training on a regular schedule and participating in exercises and other activities alongside regular USAF units. This extends to major exercises like 'Red Flag' and 'Gunsmoke' and units from both second-line commands do often use the annual two-week active duty training – AcDu-Tra, more familiarly known as 'summer camp' – periods to deploy to overseas bases for 'in-theatre' familiarisation.

The USAF had planned to acquire some 750 A-10As, and production reached a peak rate of 13 aircraft a month in 1980. However, Congressional budget cuts in 1982 reduced the service's production orders to 707 aircraft, excluding the two non-standard YA-10A prototypes and the six development aircraft. Fairchild completed its last contract for A-10As in February 1984.

The end of production came about despite efforts to expand the A-10 market. Fairchild leased an A-10 from the USAF

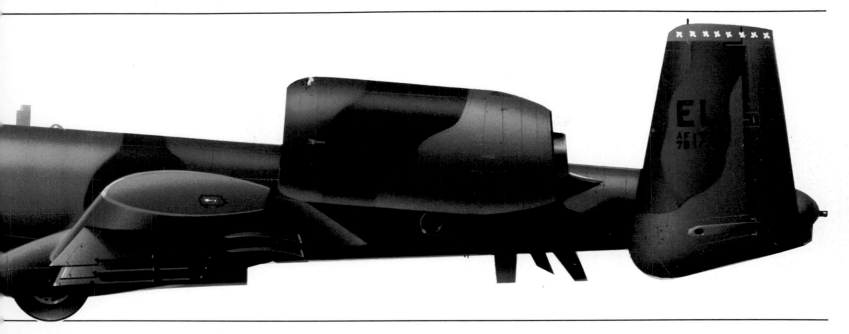

in September 1976, to make the type's first appearance outside the USA at the Farnborough Air Show. An appearance at the Paris show in the following year ended disastrously on the opening day, when the A-10 failed to complete a loop under a low cloudbase and crashed, killing its pilot. But the USAF itself had not yet devised satisfactory tactics for the A-10, and although professional observers were impressed by the power of the GAU-8/A, little serious interest was forthcoming.

Two-seat A-10s

The longest and most costly campaign was aimed at developing the A-10 into a specialized night/adverse weather (N/AW) attack aircraft. While the USAF had no stated requirement for such an aircraft, there was enough interest to persuade Fairchild that a full-scale demonstration programme would be worthwhile. In late 1977 the company began to discuss such a programme with the USAF and avionics suppliers, and work started in April 1978, supported by USAF research and development money, Fairchild company funds and contributions of time and materiel from interested avionics suppliers.

The demonstrator was based on the first of the A-10 development aircraft, and the modification took only 13 months, the N/AW aircraft making its first flight on

May 4, 1979. Provision for a second seat had been made in the original design: the second cockpit occupied the space above the ammunition drum, displacing a few avionics boxes, which were relocated in the fairing behind the canopy. The fins were increased in height by 20in (51cm) to compensate for the extra side area, but the airframe was otherwise unchanged. The two-seater could be flown from either cockpit, with the elevated rear seat and back-up flight controls.

The most important feature of the aircraft, though, was a pair of pods housing a suite of avionic subsystems. Assembled from proven and available components, these were designed to allow precision attacks at night, en route navigation in weather at low level and, to some extent, precision attacks in adverse weather.

Equipment on the N/AW demonstrator included a modified Westinghouse WX-50 radar in an underwing pod. Based on a standard weather radar, it was modified to act as a short-range, multi-mode navigation and attack radar. It had three functions: simple mapping, terrain-avoidance and attack, and as an attack radar it was capable of picking out small moving targets on the ground. The second pod, on the centreline pylon, contained a Texas Instruments AAR-42 Flir and a Ferranti 105 laser designator,

on a single mounting which could be steered to search for targets. A forward-looking low-light TV system was mounted in place of the Pave Penny sensor, and a Litton LN-39 inertial navigation system completed the suite. The avionics fed a modified Kaiser A-10 HUD and a pair of cathode-ray-tube (CRT) displays in the rear cockpit.

The system was much simpler than that on a fast-mover night strike aircraft such as the F-111, because it was not automatic; with only half the speed, it did not need to be. And because it was not directly controlling the aircraft, the navigation/attack system did not have to be designed to be fully operational after a major failure, the single biggest complicating factor in the F-111 systems. The pilot flew the aircraft at all times, with the help of terrain-following radar (TFR) and Flir data, superimposed on the HUD to give a single picture with limited depth cues. The back-seat weapons system operator (WSO) would use the INS for en route navigation, and could use the Flir to search for targets to either side of the track; in that case, the pilot would use LLTV in place of Flir.

The WSO would operate guided weapons, and the pilot would carry out gun attacks. The concept of the two-seat aircraft was that the WSO would search for a second target as the pilot attacked the first. The WSO would enter its exact

coordinates on the INS, and the pilot would follow INS instructions for an accurate, first-pass attack. The laser would be used for accurate ranging and to designate targets for laser-guided bomb attacks.

The demonstrator was extensively evaluated during 1979-82, and just under 300 hours of testing proved that precision night attack was possible with the simple sensor fit. Fairchild proposed a production version, with the Flir and radar built into the landing gear pods, and the laser and LLTV installations buried in the wing leading edge. Avionics integration would have been more refined than on the 'breadboard' prototype. The N/AW aircraft would also have had a cleaner one-piece windshield and a single clamshell canopy, and the rear cockpit would have been protected by alloy/titanium/nylon side panels.

Night attack options

The N/AW A-10 would have cost $1.5 million more than the standard A-10A, and in 1979 Fairchild was offering new-built aircraft for delivery in early 1983. In retrospect, it is clear that this would have provided the USAF with a versatile nocturnal interdiction type much more quickly than any other programme. Fairchild also offered a number of cheaper options based on the demonstrator programme. One of these was a single-seat night attack (SSNA) configuration, with underwing Flir/laser and radar pods, as on the demonstrator, modified HUD and two head-down multifunction CRTs. There was also an 'austere' SSNA version with no radar, but with Flir/laser pod and INS for night attack on targets of known location, and an austere two-seater.

Unfortunately, all these A-10 variants were designed to do the same job as Lantirn, which was still scheduled to be available before 1985. Lantirn promised a great many advantages. Its high-technology features, such as its automatic target recognition system and advanced HUD, would provide all the performance of the fully-equipped two-seater, through a simple modification of the single-seat aircraft; one of the USAF's biggest reservations about the N/AW programme was that the WSO represented superfluous weight and cost on daytime missions and in some night operations in clear air. Lantirn, too, could be applied to the F-16 and F-15 as well as to the A-10.

Most of the USAF's testing of the de-

Left: Four A-10s of the 917th TFW, based at Barksdale AFB, Louisiana, participating in AFRES Aerials exercises over Texas.

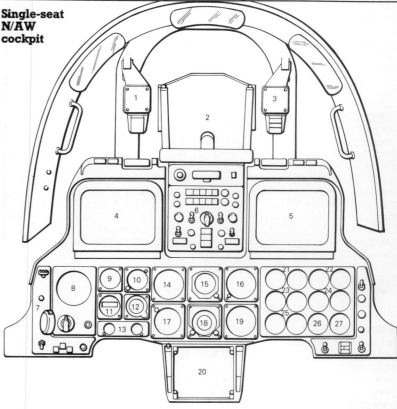

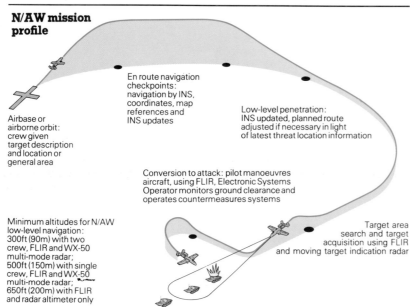

N/AW mission profile

Airbase or airborne orbit: crew given target description and location or general area

En route navigation checkpoints: navigation by INS, coordinates, map references and INS updates

Low-level penetration: INS updated, planned route adjusted if necessary in light of latest threat location information

Conversion to attack: pilot manoeuvres aircraft, using FLIR, Electronic Systems Operator monitors ground clearance and operates countermeasures systems

Minimum altitudes for N/AW low-level navigation:
300ft (90m) with two crew, FLIR and WX-50 multi-mode radar;
500ft (150m) with single crew, FLIR and WX-50 multi-mode radar;
650ft (200m) with FLIR and radar altimeter only

Target area search and target acquisition using FLIR and moving target indication radar

Single-seat N/AW cockpit

The cockpit proposed by Fairchild for the radar-equipped single-seat night attack A-10 would have allowed both fixed and moving targets to be attacked at night in low to moderate threat areas; an austere version without radar was also offered, as well as the two-seater.

1 Acceleration indicator
2 Head-up display
3 Standby compass
4 Left multifunction display
5 Right multifunction display
6 Display controls
7 Landing controls
8 Fuel quantity indicator
9 Angle of attack indicator
10 Clock
11 Channel frequency indicator
12 Standby attitude indicator
13 Hydraulics systems indicators
14 Airspeed indicator
15 Attitude director indicator
16 Barometric altitude indicator
17 Radar warning receiver azimuth indicator
18 Horizontal situation indicator
19 Vertical velocity indicator
20 Armament control panel
21 Engine temperature indicators
22 Engine fan RPM indicators
23 Engine core RPM indicators
24 Engine fuel flow indicators
25 Engine oil pressure indicators
26 Auxiliary power unit RPM indicator
27 Auxiliary power unit temperature indicator

Top: The two-seat night/adverse weather A-10 conversion prepares for a night takeoff with FLIR/laser pod under the fuselage and WX-50 radar pod under the port wing.

Above: Typical mission profile for a night/adverse weather attack in the A-10, with the avionics pods facilitating penetration, target acquisition and attack.

monstrator was dedicated to proving the service's contention that such a type could be operated successfully by a single pilot, as would be the case with Lantirn. It was not until late 1981 that the DoD decided to delay production of Lantirn until the basic principles had been proven, and by that time the opportunity for the all-weather two-seat A-10 had passed. The USAF did order 30 two-seat A-10Bs in 1981, but these were to have been combat trainers with standard cockpits. They would have been used by AFRES and ANG units, but Congress cancelled funding for these aircraft and no A-10Bs were built. Fairchild did try to find export markets for the A-10 – such as Morocco, the target of extensive presentations – but the type was hampered by specialization; with fighter unit costs climbing towards $20 million, few potential customers could afford economically sized fleets unless they standardized on a single type. The A-10's inability to take on the air-to-air role was apparent, while its sleek supersonic competitors could, at least, make an impressive show of putting bombs or A-model Mavericks on to simulated targets.

Export attempt
The last battle to save the A-10 was mounted in 1982-83, when the type was proposed to several nations as a multi-role 'flying artillery' system, useful against many targets other than tanks. Following the Falklands war, Fairchild pushed the use of the A-10 as a maritime strike aircraft, particularly in areas such as South-East Asia. Equipped with the WX-50 radar, already tested on the N/AW demonstrator, and exploiting its long endurance, the A-10 could have proved a useful maritime strike weapon, carrying missiles such as Harpoon or Exocet. Air battles in the Falklands and Middle East, too, had shown the effectiveness of the new 'point-and-shoot' AIM-9L missile, and Fairchild's simulations demonstrated that the A-10 would defeat most opponents if armed with a weapon in that class.

At the 1983 Paris Air Show, Fairchild salesmen did their best to sound optimistic. Three customers, two in the Middle East and one in South-East Asia, were leading candidates for A-10 sales. The type was seen as a useful complement to an interceptor such as the F-5E, and Fairchild expected to sell 70-80 aircraft in 1983-85. At the same time, in Washington, the company and its Congressional friends were making a final and unsuccessful attempt to reverse the 1982 production cutback and keep the line open until export orders could be secured.

One Fairchild man at Paris gave a penetrating analysis of the factors favouring and hampering his company's sales efforts. "Essentially, our competitors are fighters which could cost twice as much as an A-10," he told Dave Griffiths of the US publication *Defense Week*, but went on to define what was probably the A-10's biggest negative in the export market: "Of course, a Mach 2 plane is sexier, and some pilots may think hitting ground targets is a grunt's job." Even more accurately, the executive added: "If there were any armies in the world that had their own tactical aviation, they'd love the A-10." Unhappily for Fairchild, and, perhaps, unhappily for the 'grunt' in the field, soldiers seldom if ever have any say in buying fighters.

Warthogs at war
Years later, the A-10A looked like being a major casualty of the so-called 'peace dividend', for it was one of the first types to be selected for withdrawal from Europe in the wake of warmer East-West relationships and a sudden outbreak of democracy to the east of what had once been the 'Iron Curtain'.

With a Conventional Forces Agreement concluded and with much Soviet armour due to be withdrawn, some reduction in the size of the European-based A-10 fleet was understandable and logical but it appears that it was destined to be removed en masse, being, if anything, more a victim of antipathy among the more elevated levels of the USAF hierarchy than of any lack of ability that it possessed. For the A-10, though, that had long been the way of things, with those responsible for policy and planning evidently being far from certain about just what it could do – or, even, about what it was designed to do.

It was to take a war to force a reappraisal but the A-10 and its pilots seized the opportunity to demonstrate precisely what they were capable of. As will be seen, that was more than just killing armoured fighting vehicles. . .

The August 1990 invasion and annexation of Kuwait by Iraq very quickly prompted Saudi Arabia to look to the West for assistance to forestall the threat of still more military adventures by Saddam Hussein. That assistance wasn't slow in coming and nor was it slow to recognise the danger posed by Iraq's armoured might, for the A-10A Thunderbolt was soon winging its way eastward, along with other sexier elements of US air power.

Invasion of Kuwait
Initially, TAC was the sole source of deploying Warthogs, despatching aircraft from the 23rd and 354th TFWs within weeks of the invasion. Deployment got under way in August and these two units are believed to have eventually sent about 100 examples between them. Later, as Allied air power expanded to extraordinary lengths, other major USAF commands also contributed as the number of A-10s in the Gulf rose to around the 150 mark.

New arrivals began reaching the theatre in late December and early January and included more from TAC, which sent a number of OA-10s from the 602nd TACW (Tactical Air Control Wing). USAFE also chipped in with a squadron's worth (the 511th TFS) from Alconbury just a couple of days after Christmas 1990 and even AFRES got in on the act by mobilising the New Orleans-based 706th TFS for Gulf duty at about the same time. The main operating base for the A-10s was King Fahd Airport near Damman, Saudi Arabia and the disparate elements were grouped together to form the 354th TFW (Provisional).

Once the fighting began, however, many A-10s were dispersed to forward operating locations which included desert landing strips and even sections of highway. Minimal support facilities –

primarily fuel and munitions – were available, and use of these sites significantly reduced transit times to the battlefield area. In so doing, it allowed the A-10 force to react more rapidly than would have been possible had it operated solely from Damman.

It is doubtful if the A-10 force had much input in the early part of the war, when Allied air power fought for air superiority by attacking Iraqi command and control facilities and air bases. Once the focus of activity shifted to Iraq's ground forces, however, the Warthog very quickly began to justify its presence by exacting a heavy toll on those forces. Ranging far and wide over Kuwait and parts of Iraq, the A-10 used its impressive firepower to lethal effect. Enemy armour and troop concentrations figured high on the target list for fairly obvious reasons, with the GAU-8/A Avenger cannon and the Maverick air-to-surface missile being particularly effective against the former.

'Dumb' bombs like the Mk.82 500-pounder and Rockeye CBUs were also extensively used against troops and armour but these were by no means the only targets, for A-10s also played a part in the effort to dismantle the formidable array of anti-aircraft weapons systems that Iraq had gathered together in Kuwait. This entailed attacking SAM sites and their associated radars as well as AAA (anti-aircraft artillery) emplacements. And, despite fairly well-defined operational objectives, there were also 'targets of opportunity', the pedestrian but 'long-legged' and heavily armed A-10 being particularly well suited for stooging around a 'kill box' and engaging almost anything that caught its pilot's eye or took his fancy.

Much of the time, the A-10 force operated in small packages, which gave them reasonable freedom of manoeuvre when operating against a specific 'kill box'. Defensive measures most commonly entailed relying on their own jamming pods as well as chaff and flares but they did also look to support from F-4G Wild Weasels for defence suppression in particularly 'hot' areas. Protection against aerial threats fell to the trusty AIM-9 Sidewinder although there is no evidence of enemy fighter aircraft being encountered by A-10s.

Forward air controllers were frequently employed in co-ordinating air strikes in support of friendly forces, these being either on the ground or in the air. Airborne FACs included Marine Corps OV-10s and Air Force OA-10s, both types that are well suited to the mission but 'fast FAC' F-16s were also active and it is reasonable to assume that these also worked with the A-10 pilots.

The ground campaign

One of the greatest problems encountered during the purely aerial phase stemmed from their initial success, for the battlefields over which they regularly flew were soon littered with dead and damaged armour and other war materiel. Since it was obviously undesirable to expend valuable ordnance on what was already little more than scrap metal, this meant that pilots had to linger longer if they were to find fresh targets, and that automatically exposed them to greater risk of being brought down by enemy fire.

Once the ground war opened, the operating philosophy almost certainly changed, with the A-10s and other tank-busters expanding the perimeter of operations and ranging out ahead of Allied ground forces so as to clear a path through which they could advance. It was during this period that they scored some of their greatest successes, perhaps best epitomised by two pilots of the 23rd TFW who between them accounted for 23 tanks on February 25 to set a new record for 'Desert Storm'.

Operations didn't end with the coming of darkness, for one squadron (the 355th TFS) specialised in fighting by night, using techniques and procedures that were developed during the run-up to war. Flying without lights, night operations were fraught with the risk of collision, but the use of different stacking heights, clearly defined reference points and much radio chat succeeded in eliminating that danger, while the muted whine of the turbofan engines often allowed the A-10s to approach and attack unobserved from the ground.

Lacking much in the way of specialised night flying kit, the Thunderbolt pilots used the AGM-65D Maverick's infra-red seeker head as the primary aid in finding targets by displaying its imagery on a scope in the cockpit. Once a target was detected, other weaponry could be brought to bear, this imaginative idea allowing the Warthog to be employed in the nightly hunt for the elusive 'Scud' missiles. Quite how successful they were in finding any missiles is hard to say, but A-10s were certainly involved in 'Scud-busting', with one high point in the war against these weapons occurring on February 27, shortly before the ceasefire. On that occasion, a member of the American special forces discovered a group of missiles just minutes before he was due to be picked up by helicopter. Alerted to the threat, A-10s and other Allied aircraft spent the best part of the next six hours reducing the site to rubble.

There were other high moments, most notably when two A-10 pilots scored air-to-air 'kills'. In both cases, the victims were helicopters. Captain Bob Swain of the 706th TFS opening the account on February 6 when he obliterated an unidentified machine (probably an MBB Bo.105 or an Alouette III) with a couple of bursts of gunfire after failing to obtain a Sidewinder lock-on. Nine days later, Captain Todd Sheeny of the 511th TFS emulated the feat and shot down a Mil Mi-8 which proved to be the 42nd and last Iraqi loss in the air-to-air battle but A-10s also managed to knock out some Iraqi warplanes on the ground.

There were also some bad moments, the very nature of war and the A-10 mission making it almost inevitable that casualties would arise. Fortunately, these were relatively few, but five Warthogs were lost to enemy action during the course of 'Desert Storm'. The first victim was Captain Richard Storr who encountered extremely accurate AAA fire on February 2 although he ejected and was eventually released from captivity on March 5.

For the A-10 community, February 14 was certainly a black day, with two aircraft being shot down while engaging Republican Guard armour in north-west Kuwait. Both pilots were from the 353rd TFS, but their fortunes differed markedly, First Lieutenant Robert Sweet surviving to be released on March 5, while Captain Steven Phillis is still listed as missing in action. Five days later, Lieutenant Colonel Jeffrey Fox of the 23rd TASS (Tactical Air Support Squadron) tangled with a SAM while on a FAC mission but he too managed to escape from his wrecked OA-10A, only to be captured and eventually freed. Finally, First Lieutenant Patrick Olson was killed in action in unexplained circumstances shortly before the end of the war.

Losses like those were hard to take, as indeed were two separate incidents in which A-10s opened fire on friendly ground forces. The first such occurrence came during the battle for Khafji on or about January 29 when 11 US Marines died in a light armoured vehicle, subsequent analysis of damage to the vehicle apparently confirming that it had been targeted by 30mm cannon fire.

Later, on February 26, nine British soldiers died when two Warriors were struck by Maverick missiles. Conflicting accounts of this incident have emerged, but it seems that both vehicles were hit by mistake following a British call for air support during intense fighting in Iraq, even though they displayed the correct identification marks and visibility was good. Tragic it undoubtedly was, but in such fast-moving situations, mishaps like that are unlikely to be avoided.

A-10 achievement

As yet, it is still too early to quote chapter and verse on the achievements of the A-10 in 'Desert Storm' but it is known that Iraq lost somewhere in the region of 4,000 armoured vehicles and there can be little doubt that the A-10 Thunderbolt II was responsible for a good proportion of that figure. Acknowlegement of its worth and a tacit admission that they had perhaps got it wrong before seems to be evident among the higher reaches of the USAF for it now appears that plans to withdraw the A-10 have been put on hold.

Indeed, it is one type that has been associated with a concept whereby the Air Force is to organise a pair of prototype 'task-orientated' Composite Air Wings in the USA by 1993. One such Wing is set to function in the role of supporting ground troops and will include examples of the A-10, F-16, AC-130 and various transport aircraft types. No location has yet been made known for this organisation but Pope AFB looks like being a good bet, since it presently accommodates a C-130 transport wing and is also part of Fort Bragg in North Carolina which serves as home to the 82nd Airborne Division.

Below: An A-10 over the Gulf, carrying an ECM pod, Maverick AGM and two AIM-9 Sidewinders.

Performance and Tactics

A-10 tactics have been constantly revised and improved to meet a changing threat, and are tailored to the unique slow-flying, quick-turning performance of the aircraft. Originally intended to loiter at medium altitudes until required, A-10s now operate at extremely low altitude to counter defensive weapons, and can fly and fight effectively under low cloud and in poor visibility. The A-10 can sustain operations from austerely equipped forward bases, and can even 'ground loiter' on a good stretch of road. The A-10 complements the US Army's attack helicopter force in action against advancing armour, and unique coordinated tactics have been developed to make the best use of all resources.

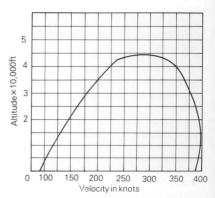

January 25, 1979, was an English winter day like most others. There was a penetratingly damp chill in the air, and the overcast hung over RAF Bentwaters like an inverted bowl of frozen porridge. It was on this uncompromisingly European day that the A-10A arrived in Europe as an operational fighting aircraft.

It is not considered gentlemanly to cast aspersions upon an ally's newest weapon system, but concern over the effectiveness of the A-10 in Europe had reached very high levels in the NATO command structure. The USAF A-10s would replace McDonnell Douglas F-4D Phantoms. These were not the newest types in service, and were certainly not designed for blind precision attacks, but they had two seats, inertial navigation systems and secondary air-

Below: An 81st TFW pilot demonstrates the Warthog's surprising agility: the same degree of manoeuvrability, translated to low levels, is the key to the A-10's ability to survive combat in high-threat areas.

defence capability, and the back-seater was available to operate the whole range of first-generation targeting pods and guided weapons.

All NATO's senior air officers had seen films of A-10s delivering deadly, accurate anti-tank attacks from the gin-clear skies of Nevada, and most of them were not convinced that the same effect could be achieved in Europe, which is dark for 19 hours of the day in winter and overcast more often than not. The same officers had been briefed on the A-10's ability to withstand multiple hits from 23mm shells; they were also well aware of the existence of the Soviet SA-8 Gecko missile system, which had made its public debut in 1975. Generally, the feeling was that the European air forces had managed to prevent the USAF from fielding the F-16 in a form ideally suited to a central front in Vietnam or, preferably, Nevada, but that they might have failed to do so in the case of the A-10.

The controversy over the A-10 has remained active, and has kept the pressure on TAC to devise effective tactics

against the changing threat, and demonstrate how they would be used in action. Certainly, the way in which the A-10 is used in training and exercises today is very different from the projections of the A-X planners. But it is also true that current A-10 tactics exploit virtually all the unique features of the aircraft; and even if some things might have been done differently had the present mission been envisaged from the outset, the A-10 is available, works well and is no sense inadequate for its mission.

The threats

The concept and design of the A-10 were based on an accurate perception of Soviet military equipment and tactics in the late 1960s. (In this, at least, the Warthog is one up on the aristocratic F-15 Eagle, which was strongly influenced by an immensely flattering assessment of the MiG-25 Foxbat). The primary attack weapon was the tank, used in large concentrations and dedicated to the advance. Unlike contemporary Western tank units, Soviet armoured

Above: Although ostensibly lacking in glamour, the A-10 mission is one of the most demanding in the USAF – and one of the most sought-after by pilots.

Flight envelope

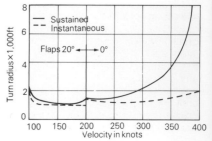

Performance graph for the A-10 in standard day conditions, at a design weight of 31,170lb (14,138kg), with six pylons fitted and at maximum thrust.

Turn performance

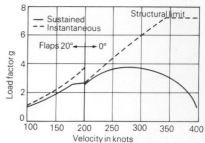

Standard day sustained and instantaneous turn rates for an A-10 with six Mk 82 bombs for a weight of 31,000lb (14,061kg) at 5,000ft (1,524m).

Load factors

Maximum load factors in standard day conditions at an altitude of 5,000ft with six Mk 82 bombs for a gross weight of 31,000lb (14,061kg).

formations carried their own air defence systems. The most formidable of these was the ZSU-23-4 Shilka, a close-range defence weapon with no direct equivalent in the West.

The Shilka is designed to run with the tanks, on a PT-76 tracked amphibious chassis. It is armed with four 23mm cannon, with a total firing rate of 4,000 rounds/min, carries a great deal of ammunition and features liquid-cooled gun barrels, so it can sustain high rates of fire over a relatively long period. Considering the effectiveness of much less sophisticated light AAA over Vietnam, it was understandable that TAC perceived the Shilka system as a prime threat in the CAS arena long before its combat debut in 1973.

The threat from Soviet aircraft was not considered to be much of a problem for A-X in the late 1960s. Soviet air-to-air fighters were used defensively, to protect airbases and rear-area assets. TAC's fighter squadrons were equipped to keep the skies cleared over friendly ground all the time, and over hostile ground where necessary. A-X was not intended to penetrate far beyond the FLOT (forward line of own troops), and any encounters with MiGs would be accidental. However, the threat of aircraft or missile attack on airbases, particularly those closest to the battle line, was certainly present.

Tactical concepts

The A-10 was designed and equipped with European weather in mind, contrary to some opinion. But it was designed to cope with weather in a completely different way from an F-111 or Tornado. The theory was that zero-zero weather – no ceiling and no horizontal visibility – was not only rare but would halt all military operations, so there was no need for such extreme in-weather capability in a CAS type. Instead, the A-X was planned to operate under, rather than in, the weather and in reduced visibility.

Low ceilings and poor visibility are a cage for the fighter pilot. Unknown terrain lurks beyond the limits of visibility, and, as pilots say, the ground has a kill probability of 1.0. The ceiling is not dangerous in itself, but is a one-way exit from the air-to-ground fight. The pilot loses his target, and has to find a hole in the cloud if he is to descend and rejoin battle. The A-10 was designed to manoeuvre and fight visually within this confined space.

The A-10 is not a high-g, high-powered aircraft, but the one thing that it can do better than any supersonic fighter is turn at low speeds. A fighter like the F-16 is designed to catch a victim or lose an attacker in a turn, and does it with brute power installed in the lightest possible airframe. Low speeds represent loss of energy, and are avoided at all costs. The A-10 is different in concept. Low turning airspeeds are accepted, because air combat capability is not required. Because the airspeed is low, the

Above: Medium-altitude Maverick launch from the lead ship of a standard two-aircraft formation. The threat level in Europe forced a revision of the tactical concepts.

Below: From target recognition to Maverick launch takes the same time, during which the fast-mover gets much closer to the target and its associated defensive systems.

A-10/F-16 Maverick attack ranges

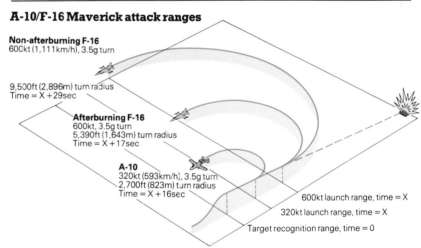

Non-afterburning F-16
600kt (1,111km/h), 3.5g turn
9,500ft (2,896m) turn radius
Time = X + 29sec

Afterburning F-16
600kt, 3.5g turn
5,390ft (1,643m) turn radius
Time = X + 17sec

A-10
320kt (593km/h), 3.5g turn
2,700ft (823m) turn radius
Time = X + 16sec

600kt launch range, time = X
320kt launch range, time = X
Target recognition range, time = 0

A-10 can attain a high rate of turn, in degrees/sec, without the high g forces that would be associated with the same rate at higher speeds. Low airspeed and high turn rate combine to give a small turning radius; the first lesson in geometry states that the circumference of the turn, the distance which the aircraft actually travels, is smaller too. The aircraft will therefore take less time to complete its turn.

Translating theory into fact, it is paradoxical but true that the A-10 will out-turn even an F-16 in full afterburner when the two aircraft are carrying similar loads. At 320kt (590km/h) and 3.5g, the A-10 can complete a half-turn, radius 2,700ft (824m), in 16 seconds. The F-16, at 600kt (1,110km/h) and 6g, makes a 3,620ft (1,043m) turn, and takes 17 seconds.

It is because of this emphasis on a quick turn rather than a fast turn that the A-10 can fight in the cage – the limited volume defined by ceiling and visibility. Early operational tests with the A-10 showed that this concept worked and that the A-10 pilot could run into the target area, identify a pinpoint target, turn and attack it under a 1,000ft (305m) ceiling, with 1.5-2 miles (2.4-3.2km) visibility. Even in a European midwinter, TAC's records showed, similar or better

conditions could be expected, on average, for eight hours a day.

By contrast, the apparently better equipped F-4D could not venture below the clouds unless the ceiling was at least 3,000ft (915m) and visibility 3 miles (4.8km). Conditions that good are encountered, on average, only four hours a day in midwinter, and only six hours a day from the beginning of November to the end of February. And as any European knows, the daily weather pattern does not conform to some arbitrary seasonal average. The difference between the A-10 and the fast mover could amount to weeks on end in which the A-10 would be the only aircraft that could attack ground targets at all.

Another objective set down by the original A-X philosophy was quick reaction, to be attained by a number of means. Airborne loiter was among the most important. The A-10 was designed to be launched from a relatively safe base, 250nm (460km) behind the battle line, and loiter for two hours before carrying out an attack. This meant that the A-10 could, in theory, be used on the 'cab-rank' principle developed by the 2nd Tactical Air Force in Western Europe in 1944-45. A-10s would be launched at regular intervals and join a loose traffic pat-

Below: Medium-altitude loiter, World War II style, was out of the question in the context of NATO's Central Front, but could still have applications in low-threat environments.

Designed close air support mission

1.88hr loiter
174kt (322km/h)
5,000ft (1,524m)

Return cruise at 286kt (530km/h) and 35,000ft (10,668m)

10min combat
300kt (556km/h)
at sea level

20min sea level loiter at 130kt (241km/h)

Cruise out at 296kt (549km/h) and 25,000ft (7,620m)

250nm (463km)

Takeoff weight 46,196lb (20,954kg)
18 Mk 82 LDGP bombs, max 30mm ammunition

Terrain following at high and low speeds

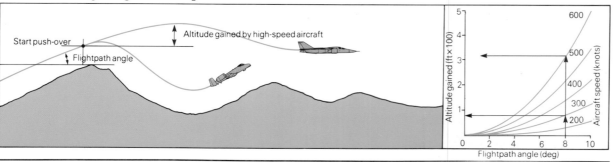

tern, the 'cab-rank', behind the battle line. They could respond immediately to any call for support, while other A-10s would be launched to relieve aircraft on the rank after their two hours on station expired.

In combat, the A-10 was designed to be relatively invulnerable to light AAA or shoulder-fired SAMs. Heavier SAMs presented a different type of threat. In the late 1960s these did not travel with the main armoured force, and if they were encountered in the CAS zone, would have been emplaced in a hurry. Moreover, the A-10's manoeuvrability would enable it to stay below the minimum altitudes of such weapons, and inside their minimum range, as it roamed around the battlefield shooting tanks.

The foregoing represents a brief summary of A-10 tactics as they were envis-

Above: While the A-10 at 300kt (555km/h) gains a modest 80ft (24m) in the push-over, an F-111 in hard-ride terrain-following mode climbs a dangerous 330ft (100m).

SA-8 avoidance tactics

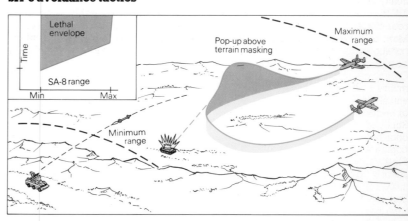

Left: The deployment of the Soviet SA-8 surface-to-air-missile with armoured columns contributed to a major rethink of CAS tactics.

Above: The A-10 returns to terrain masking after the attack in less time than it takes the SA-8 to acquire its target, lock on and launch.

ZSU-23-4 avoidance tactics

3sec linear flight path from start track to cease fire; open fire after 1.5sec

1sec TOF

3sec TOF

5sec TOF

Start track

Cease fire

TOF: Time of flight of ZSU-23-4 projectile

Above: Manoeuvrability at low altitudes allows the A-10 to exploit natural cover to the full, allowing air defences only the briefest glimpse of its armoured form.

aged in the early days of the programme. It is probably fair to say that most of them were completely invalidated by the time the A-10 came to Europe at the beginning of 1979. There were at least three critical factors which were not anticipated in the formulation of the A-X requirement, and between them they have made life a great deal more difficult for the A-10.

New threats
One factor was the performance of the ZSU-23-4. It was known to be a dangerous system, but its lethality was not fully appreciated until the Arab-Israeli war of 1973. The projectile is nearly twice as heavy as that of the M61A-1 Vulcan, at 0.41lb (0.19kg), and muzzle velocity is a respectable 3,200ft/sec (970m/sec). More importantly, however, the barrel cooling and other features give the four-barrel mount a very low dispersion. Combined with the sustained 4,000rds/min rate of fire, this makes the ability to withstand one or two 23mm strikes more or less academic. Like the GAU-8/A, the Shilka tends to hit its targets more than once or twice, and the effects have been compared to those of a rotary saw. The Shilka's effectiveness drops off very sharply beyond about 3,000-3,300ft (920-1,000m), but this certainly does not mean that the threat which it poses can be ignored.

The West got another unpleasant surprise in 1975, with the unveiling of the Soviet SA-8 Gecko mobile SAM system. Western experts had expected the Soviet Union to field a new short-range SAM. It would be much more effective

than a pursuit-course heat-seeking weapon, but it would be more mobile than the bigger SA-6 system, which is carried on two vehicles, and it would have a shorter minimum range and lower minimum altitude. Everyone assumed, though, that the Soviets would design a small, simple system like the Roland or Rapier. Instead, they adapted the design of a sophisticated naval missile, the SA-N-4.

The SA-8 is a heavy, complex system, indicating its importance in Soviet planning and tactics. Mounted on a specially developed 25-30 ton (27.5-33 tonne) wheeled vehicle, the SA-8 system is complete with surveillance and tracking radar, and two independent high-power, narrow-beam radio command links. If radar is jammed or ineffective for other reasons, SA-8 has an electro-optical tracking and guidance system, and according to some sources the missile may have infra-red terminal homing. The round is considerably larger than those used by Western fully mobile systems, and carries a 110lb (50kg) blast-fragmentation warhead. The initial SA-8 configuration carried four missiles, but the improved SA-8B carries six, in sealed box launchers.

A third unexpected development was the extremely rapid introduction into service of the MiG-23 Flogger B/G fighter. The MiG-23 itself had been seen in 1967, but Western intelligence – hypnotised by the MiG-25 – failed to appreciate its importance to Soviet tactical airpower. Production accelerated at breakneck speed in 1972-75, in parallel with development of its new radar and missile armament. Not a dogfighter, but fast, heavily armed and comprehensively equipped, Flogger B/G is the first Soviet fighter designed to carry the air war into NATO's territory, beyond the reach of ground control.

The effect of these three developments on planned A-10 tactics was profound. The A-10 pilot was supposed to identify and select his target on the first pass, keep it in sight in a tight turn and attack on a second pass. Against Shilkas and SA-8s, this would be suicide. The aggressive MiG-23, meanwhile, put an end to the absolute security of airspace over friendly ground: so much for loiter and transit at medium altitudes. Between 1975 and 1979 the ground rules of A-10 operation were completely rewritten to cope with the changing threats while still exploiting the unique attributes of the aircraft. The changes affected survival and defensive tactics, attack profiles and targeting, and operational deployment.

Tactics for survival
Survivability has been at the centre of the A-10 controversy. The aircraft has most often been criticized on account of its speed. Most NATO strike aircraft are designed to attack at speeds of 600kt

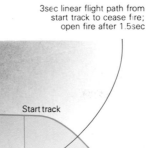

Left: At GAU-8/A range, the Warthog can carry out its attack and be back under the Shilka's minimum elevation before the deadly stream of 23mm projectile can reach it.

Below left: The ZSU-23-4, seen here in Polish army service, was always considered a major threat, but its lethality was not fully appreciated until the 1973 Arab-Israeli war.

(1,110km/h); the A-10 attacks at barely more than half that speed, being capable of 325kt (602km/h) with a typical weapons load. TAC and Fairchild contend, however, that when the A-10 is properly used it can survive against Soviet defensive systems, and fare better than other aircraft. Tactics have presumably been evaluated not only against simulated Soviet systems on the USAF's Nevada ranges, but also against the real thing: captured SA-8s and Shilkas, and clandestinely obtained MiG-23s, are all believed to be in use.

The first point made by the A-10's advocates is that in the battle area, where the A-10s operate, the air defence system is not operating at peak efficiency. Firing positions will have been selected under pressure, on unfamiliar ground, and fields of fire of the different systems will not overlap in the optimum pattern. Communications, command and control will all be degraded to some extent. Even the advancing second echelon is subject to similar pressures.

Another important observation is that a Mach 0.9 speed is not a primary defence against a Mach 2.3 missile, let alone a Mach 3 shell. The only benefit of speed itself is to reduce the time in which an aircraft is exposed to defensive systems on a given flightpath. It is also a factor in generating high crossing rates relative to the defensive weapon's sightline.

Under some circumstances, higher speed may actually militate against the best defensive tactic, which is to interpose a hill between the gun or SAM system and the target. TAC has been a late but enthusiastic convert to the doctrine of very-low-level flight, and A-10 units are the command's leading exponents of the tactic. Once again, it is the A-10's ability to manoeuvre hard at low airspeeds that is important. Cruising at its normal and most efficient speed, the A-10 can make sharp flightpath changes without incurring as much g as a faster aircraft following the same trajectory. Clearing the top of a hill, the A-10 will have less upward momentum than the faster aircraft, and can descend more rapidly on the other side without en-

Below: Warthog pilots do not consider MiGs a major threat: they can turn more quickly, and their guns are very effective against aircraft.

Survival against interceptors

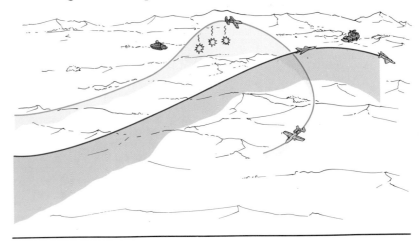

Battlefield air support mission

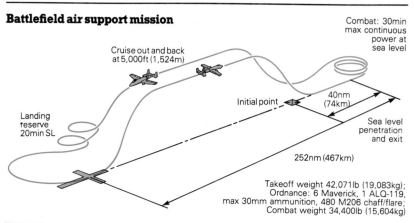

Cruise out and back at 5,000ft (1,524m)

Combat: 30min max continuous power at sea level

Landing reserve 20min SL

Initial point

40nm (74km)

Sea level penetration and exit

252nm (467km)

Takeoff weight 42,071lb (19,083kg); Ordnance: 6 Maverick, 1 ALQ-119, max 30mm ammunition, 480 M206 chaff/flare; Combat weight 34,400lb (15,604kg)

Above: Revised A-10 tactics emphasise sea-level penetration and combat in the face of the intense air defenses likely to be encountered.

Right: In battle, this would almost certainly be an opposing tank commander's last view of an A-10 – or anything else.

countering excessive levels of negative g. (Faster aircraft can, of course, roll inverted and pull their way around the top of the hill under positive g, but this tactic is only recommended if you are absolutely certain that the terrain does fall away on the opposite side of the crest.)

The A-10's small turning radius gives it a wider choice of tracks across uneven terrain which may not give a faster aircraft room to change course, and its low speed gives the pilot more time to plan the next manoeuvre. Light and natural handling takes a further weight off the pilot's mind.

At these low speeds, the A-10 can actually pull higher g than an F-16 in similar trim. When both aircraft are loaded for anti-armour operations, the A-10 can sustain a 3.25g turn at 250-300kt (460-555km/h). The F-16 can only match this performance with the use of reheat, and on dry thrust can manage only 2-2.5g in the same speed range. On dry thrust it can match the A-10's performance only by speeding up above 400kt (740km/h) and accepting a larger turning radius.

It is true that a fast-mover attack aircraft can follow terrain at reduced speeds and emulate some of the A-10's tactics. The snag is that only the A-10 and its engines are designed for such speeds. Fast-movers do not usually reduce their speed, because by doing so they drop out of their efficient cruising regime and suffer unacceptable warload/radius penalties. It is this consideration that makes the A-10's performance unique.

A-10s have been operated successfully by service pilots at average altitudes of 100ft (30m) above ground level, although most training is carried out at higher altitudes, mainly because of peacetime restrictions. Slightly higher altitudes are acceptable where the threat comes from Floggers rather than SAMs, but on the final run to the target the A-10s fly substantially lower than any other fixed-wing aircraft.

Low-level operation protects the A-10 in a number of ways. Simply concealing the aircraft for as long as possible from the sightline of the defensive system is one of them. Fairchild studies show that in hilly terrain, such as the Fulda Gap in West Germany, a ZSU-23-4 can engage targets in just 22 per cent of the area covered by its effective range if the target stays below 200ft (61m).

Again, one of the defender's advantages is the ability to see and identify the attcking aircraft before its pilot can pick out a SAM or gun system among ground clutter and other targets, but this 'first-look' advantage can be wiped out if the aircraft breaks cover at close quarters. With radar-guided or command-guided systems such as the SA-8, low flying also reduces the SAM's advantage due to

greater maximum range. Also, such weapons are not 'fire and forget' – they need a certain amount of time to lock on, fire a missile and guide it to the target. Breaking ground cover at the last moment, and returning to it as soon as possible, gives the operator the shortest possible time to engage the target.

Even with a target in sight, extremely low altitudes present problems for SAMs. Simple IR-homing SAMs have to be launched at a minimum elevation angle, because of their short range and their tendency to fly into the ground. Their effective envelope is shaped like an inverted cone with its apex at the launch point, and the lower an aircraft flies, the shorter its flightpath through the cone. An aircraft flying at 300kt (555km/h), 100ft (30m) over a SAM with a 20deg minimum launch elevation – typical of unsophisticated weapons – will be in and out of the operator's launch window in less than one second.

Radar-guided SAMs have other limitations, and can be confused by a very-low-altitude target. Radar signals bounce off a target in all directions, and will be reflected again when they strike the ground. Usually, such echoes will be well outside the narrow cone of a missile tracking beam, and will not be detected by the radar's receiver. But if the aircraft's altitude is less than twice the width of the beam, the ground echoes will be close enough to create false targets on the radar screen. Multiple echoes are another problem which increases with low altitude.

Operation at very low altitudes also protects the A-10, to some extent, from 'snapdown' attacks by MiG-23s or similar aircraft firing IR or semi-active radar-guided missiles from higher altitudes. The latest Flogger G variant is considered to have "some look-down/shoot-down capability" according to the US Department of Defense, and this implies that its High Lark radar and AA-7 Apex missile would be of limited use against a small target 100ft (30m) off the ground.

IR missiles such as the AA-8 Aphid, also carried by the MiG-23, are probably of little use against an A-10 at a lower altitude than the launch aircraft. Such all-aspect IR missiles home on the heat energy generated by friction between an airframe and the air. The A-10 is slow and relatively small, and is therefore a weak target, and the sensitivity of an IR missile is limited; if the seeker is too sensitive, it will lock on to false targets on the ground. While low-level operation does not provide a complete defence against fighters, it does mean that if the MiG-23s want to shoot down the A-10s they probably have to come down to the A-10's level to do it.

The main disadvantage of low-level operation is probably the great stress

Low-level gunnery

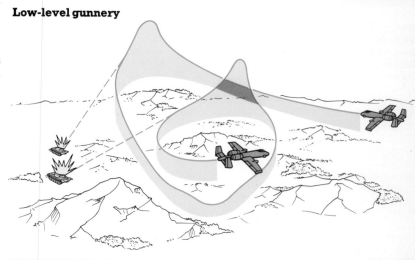

Above: Spending most of its time less than 100ft (30m) above the ground, the A-10 pops up to between 200ft (60m) and 500ft (150m) to destroy tanks with brief bursts of gunfire.

Below: The same terrain-masking and three-dimensional jinking are employed in the run-up to a Maverick delivery from 500ft (150m); a cloud base of 1,000ft (300m) is no problem.

Low-level Maverick delivery

which it places on the pilot. This has been a major factor in the abandonment of the cab-rank loiter concept. Loitering at medium altitudes is unsafe, but the physical and mental demands of flight among the treetops at 300kt (555km/h) make it inadvisable to add two hours to the mission. At that point, pilot fatigue could become a limiting factor on a squadron's ability to sustain its readiness to fight.

In combat, the A-10 is to survive partly by means of its manoeuvrability, and partly by its ability to counter-attack, with the help of its built-in and podded EW and decoys. The basic attack manoeuvre in the SA-8 era is the pop-up, or, in TAC argot, the 'bunt-up', in which the aircraft emerges from the protection of terrain, engages its target, attacks and dives back into cover.

Once again, the most important characteristic is not high speed, but low exposure time; if it is shorter than the time that the SA-8 takes to engage and hit the target, the missile operator can do nothing. The A-10's ability to manoeuvre in small radii and short time is its main asset here. Its lower speed means that it can drop back into cover at a higher descent rate than a fast jet: in a bunt, or negative-g pushover, the limiting factor is pilot tolerance rather than aircraft power, so the g force will be the same, and the slower aircraft will follow a steeper and shorter downward trajectory.

Speed is also of secondary importance in avoiding hits after a weapon has been fired at the aircraft, because any sophisticated defensive system can measure speed accurately and compensate for it. (In deference to the fast mover, it should be noted that sheer speed does reduce the time in which the target is within the lethal envelope, all other things being equal.) In the case of guns and radar-guided SAMs, however, it is possible to 'generate miss distance'. Translated, this means that when the projectile arrives where the fire-control system says the target ought to be, it is safest for the target to be somewhere else.

A common weakness of both guns and command-guided SAMs is that they work on a projection of where the target will be in one or two seconds' time, rather than shooting at its present position. This is commonsense in the case of the gun, with its dumb, unguided projectile, and less obvious in the case of the missile; but even the missile system takes a finite amount of time to detect the movement of the target, process the movement into a command signal and transmit it to the missile. Then, the missile control surfaces move, and – not quite immediately – the missile's flight-path will begin to change according to the target's motion. Unless some degree of prediction is built into the system, the combined delay will be enough to guide the missile behind the target.

The Shilka's fire-control system assumes that the aircraft will continue on a straight path at constant speed, and the SA-8 system probably does the same. The rate at which the target can diverge from that straight path is largely a matter of the g force which it can generate: in this case, the important parameter is instantaneous, short-period g rather than sustained g, because evading instant destruction is a great deal more important than preserving energy or avoiding a stall. Loaded for air-to-ground operations, the A-10 can pull as much instantaneous g as most other aircraft.

In the case of the gun, the miss distance will be a function of g and the firing

Left: Even during the brief periods when the A-10 might be exposed to fire, its structure makes it uniquely able to survive major damage.

range. At 300kt (460km/h), and with a five-second flight time for the shell, the gun will miss by 1,310ft (400m). In a missile attack, the important factors are g and the distance between the aircraft and the missile when the manoeuvre starts. According to Fairchild figures, apparently based on SA-8 characteristics, a 4g manoeuvre, initiated when the missile is 12,000ft (3,660m) away, will cause the weapon to miss by 500ft (150m); not much, but better than nothing.

Tactics such as these would be used in conjunction with the A-10's countermeasure systems. Chaff would be dropped during a bunt-up manoeuvre, to keep multiple false returns coming into the hostile radar as the A-10 itself leaves the safety of the low-level confusion zone. The ALQ-119 pod and the chaff clouds can degrade the SA-8 command link, even if the system reverts to electro-optical tracking. Flares would be used during the bunt-up, to create similar multiple-target problems for IR missiles.

The A-10 carries no specifically defensive armament, although trials have shown that an advanced IR missile such as the AIM-9L Sidewinder would be a formidable addition to its armoury. The AIM-9L is a particularly good match for the A-10. Its critical advantage over earlier weapons is that it can lock on to a target from almost any direction. This eliminates the need for the classic tail-chase, in which the attacker tries to manoeuvre into the enemy's rear quarter. Instead, the advantage goes to the aircraft which can swing its nose on to the target most rapidly, and at low altitude this will usually be the A-10. Even without

the AIM-9L, though, the instant firepower of the GAU-8/A, coupled with the A-10's rapid turn ability, make the Warthog a dangerous beast to tackle.

In particular, the effective range of the GAU-8/A has been shown to be greater than that of the Shilka, and the USAF's A-10 weapons school at Nellis AFB teaches the use of the GAU-8/A to suppress the Soviet gun in a classic High Noon shoot-out. The attack starts with a bunt-up, which takes the A-10 to the Shilka's maximum range. The Shilka starts tracking and fires, while the A-10 simultaneously enters a three-second diving attack, including a two-second burst from the cannon. At the point which the Shilka's projectiles will reach three seconds after firing, and just before the first rounds arrive, the A-10 breaks and heads for cover, and the shells miss. By that time, the first of the 130-plus shells

fired by the A-10 will be hitting the vehicle. This tactic was first demonstrated at Nellis AFB in February 1979 against a simulated Soviet tank battalion array, including four Shilkas. Two pairs of A-10s from 422 TFW attacked the formation, killed the Shilkas and, in four minutes, killed 23 tanks.

In the air-to-air regime the A-10 is, technically speaking, unarmed, because it has no way of aiming the cannon against a rapidly crossing target. But the first A-10 pilots to engage in dissimilar air combat training simply disregarded this factor and followed their instincts, pulling the quickest possible turn and spraying the adversary with simulated GAU-8/A fire. The 'Warthog stomp' has since proved extremely effective. In 57 sorties flown by the USAF's Aggressor unit at Nellis against A-10s, the A-10s survived as long as they saw their attack-

ers. Only once, when an A-10 was attacked by two F-5Es, did an A-10 pilot even have to jettison external weapons.

In more recent Red Flag exercises, even the most manoeuvrable fighters have found it advisable to avoid close-quarters engagements with the A-10s, preferring a less effective but safer shoot-down pass from above. A-10s enjoy a special exception from the Red Flag safety rule which prohibits close-quarters head-on attacks, and are permitted to close to 1,000ft (305m) before breaking off.

In action, the A-10s would usually have the advantage of sighting the enemy first. The MiG-23's High Lark radar would give advance warning of an attack and its direction, via the A-10's radar-warning system, while the A-10 itself has no emitting devices to give its location away to a Sirena 3 or similar Soviet radar-warning

Right: Conus-based A-10 units train for worldwide deployment and a variety of threat levels: the 354th TFW uses a 300 acre (120 hectare) wooded area of its South Carolina base for realistic training for Europe.

device. The aircraft are difficult to spot against the ground in their subfusc green finish – one operational problem is that A-10 pilots have been known to lose sight of their wingmen – while any attacker will be outlined against the sky. The problems presented by snap-down attacks against the A-10 have already been mentioned, so any combat will take place at low level. In all, according to Brig. Gen. Rudolph Wacker, the commander of the Europe-based A-10 force in August 1979, "At the altitudes we expect to fly, enemy interceptors pose almost a negligible threat. Interestingly,' he continued, "a careless interceptor pilot quickly changes from the hunter to hunted, and generally will find himself outmanoeuvred by the A-10, and always outgunned."

Trained in low-level tactics, schooled to take advantage of every chink in the defences, and equipped with their jamming and decoy suites, the A-10 units have become confident that their ability to survive is as great as that of any other system in clear air above a European battlefield. The controversy over the A-10 has receded, and its unique place within the NATO Central Region line-up is beginnng to be appreciated.

In current thinking, the most important of the A-10's attributes is its ability to sustain combat. Against armour, its firepower is more than twice that of any other aircraft in the TAC inventory. With 1,174 GAU-8/A rounds and six Mavericks, the A-10 can deliver 16 lethal anti-armour attacks in a single mission, or even more given efficient use of the GAU-8/A. No other type can deliver more than six Mavericks, or is armed with an effective anti-armour gun.

The A-10 can also stay in combat longer than other types, even though they may appear to have a superior range on paper. As noted earlier, an A-10 can sustain a higher turn rate than an F-16 with a comparable ordnance load, unless the

Above: During annual Thunderhog exercises, the 354th TFW uses its 'European' environment to simulate deployment, complete with all supporting elements, to austere forward operating locations.

Right and below: A-10s are also based in Alaska with the 18th TFS, 343rd Composite Wing, at Eielson AFB. During Exercise Cool Snow Hog 82-1, held at Kotzebue Air Station, this Warthog was given an unusual black and white paint scheme for evaluation purposes during the period of the exercise. The A-10s in Alaska provide the primary air support for the US Army's ground forces stationed in the Alaska defence region in the far north.

F-16 uses reheat; but the use of reheat is highly demanding of fuel. Again, with a comparable ordnance load and the same mission profile, the F-16 comes close to the A-10's radius of action, but only if it uses dry thrust exclusively in the combat area. Two minutes of combat afterburner are enough to cut the F-16's operational radius to 60 per cent of the A-10's. Four minutes of afterburner, and the F-16 can go only 40 per cent as far. With its typical anti-armour ordnance load, an ALQ-119 pod, a full load of 480 decoys and full internal fuel, the A-10 can fly 252nm (466km) to the target, including 40nm (74km) at low level, and remain in the fight, on full power, for 30 minutes.

While that mission is an indicator of the A-10's performance, it is not typical of the way the A-10 would be used in service, because one of the type's other attributes – an unusual one, but not quite unique – gives the commander a better option. The quality in queston is the A-10's ability to operate from short strips and rudimentary bases. Supersonic fighters, in general, still need 8,000-10,000ft (2,440-3,050m) of concrete for normal operations. The A-10, with full fuel and weapons, can take off in 3,600ft (1,097m) and land in 1,140ft (347m).

The landing distance is particularly significant. Combined with the A-10's slow approach speed and docile hand-ling, it means that the aircraft can be recovered safely on a short strip with a large safety margin. Even with reduced hydraulic power, no flaps or a fatigued pilot, the A-10 can recover to a 4,000ft (1,200m) strip with no trouble at all, and without using an emergency arrester hook.

Forward operating locations

At the same time, the A-10's simplicity, and the absence of any critical non-mechanical systems, means that the aircraft can not only operate from dispersed bases, which most aircraft can do, but can also sustain operations from such bases, which is a rare ability in-deed. In Europe, the A-10s are based in England, well behind the battle line, in an efficient, consolidated organisation. They would operate in wartime, however, from a group of six bases 100nm (185km) from the old West German border: from north to south, Ahlhorn, Norvenich, Sembach and Leipheim, plus two more bases which are not revealed. These forward operating locations (FOLs) have stocks of fuel, ammunition and Mavericks, together with a few of the most important spares.

With most aircraft, an attempt to sustain operations from an austere base would rapidly result in an airfield full of damaged and defective airframes

Top: Pilots of the 511th TFS, are briefed before a mission during the Cold Fire 83 exercise at Wiesbaden Air Base, Germany, in September 1983.

Above: Off-loading a Maverick from a 511th TFS A-10 after a Cold Fire 83 training mission. A total of 18 aircraft were deployed to Wiesbaden in support of the German army's Brave Lions exercise.

Left: A 511th TFS pilot at the end of a Cold Fire mission. Cold Fire and Brave Lion both formed part of the annual Autumn Forge series of combined NATO manoeuvres in Germany.

250nm (463km) nearer the battle line than the spares and people needed to repair them. The A-10's simplicity and survivability features change the picture. A hit, or close miss, which would send a more complex and less resilient aircraft down for extensive repairs may well simply pepper the A-10's secondary structure, calling for nothing more than a few temporary patches. Again, a less survivable aircraft might regain a friendly base after being hit, but might not be airworthy enough to be flown back to its home base. A maintenance team must be dispatched, to fix it for the flight home, before the main work of repair can even start. Experience has shown that the A-10 can, under the same circumstances, often ferry itself back from the FOL to the main base.

The FOL has several major advantages. It is an effective and more efficient substitute for airborne loiter in decreasing reaction time; not only are the FOLs close to the front line, but the force is

Left: A-10s line up for take-off. The aircraft's survivability allows for operations in frontline areas.

Below: The rolling plains of northern Germany are ideal tank country: they are also ideal Warthog territory, especially when winter weather grounds other types for days on end.

spread out so that no part of the line is very far from A-10 support. Because the FOL is closer to the front line than any main base, it takes less time for the A-10s to return to base, rearm and rejoin the fight, so more sorties can be flown in a day. A related benefit is a reduction of pilot flying time and fatigue for each mission.

FOL basing also makes the force less vulnerable to counter-airfield attack, for a number of reasons. Splitting the fleet among a number of FOLs forces the enemy to carry out several raids against less valuable targets. Not only that, but it is more difficult to deny an airfield to A-10s than it is to close it to fast-mover operations. The A-10s can operate from half a runway, or from a long taxiway, while their lower landing and take-off speeds mean that runway repairs need not be completed to the same standard.

Also, the FOLs can, if necessary, be covertly changed and concealed. The A-10 is an easy aircraft to fly, and operations from an unfamiliar field would present no prblems. It uses only one piece of specialized ground equipment, the ammunition loader, and supplies held at the FOL are, in general, compact and limited. Changing the position of a FOL does not, for example, call for the movement of dozens of spare engines.

Using FOLs close to the battle line, A-10 units have demonstrated their abil-

ity to fly more sorties per aircraft per day than any other type in the inventory. In early tests of the FOL concept, in April 1978, A-10s averaged nearly 15 missions per day over a three-day period and surge rates above 10 sorties have been attained in later exercises. The average sortie surge rate, though, is above six missions per day, greater than that of any other USAF aircraft.

Firepower, endurance, short reaction time, resistance to counter-air attacks and high sortie rates make the A-10 force a unique asset. Live exercises and studies have repeatedly shown that the A-10 not only performs better than other systems in its own specialized arena, but does many things which no other weapon can do at all. For example, a secondary mission assigned to the 81st TFW is to escort the USAF's combat rescue helicopters, should they have to penetrate hostile territory in the daytime. Armed with cluster weapons and the cannon to suppress groundfire, the A-10's endurance and speed make it a much more suitable escort than any other fighter.

To the ground commander or forward air controller (FAC) the A-10's 'combat persistence' is, perhaps, its salient advantage. The fast-mover strike aircraft, with its limited endurance, may be able to respond quickly to a call for help, but the support which it can offer is not

only limited in duration, but also tied to a certain time. The FAC knows that the F-16 strike requested some time ago will arrive at 1543 hours precisely, and the activities of other systems on the battlefield must be geared to that time. The A-10, by contrast, can be held in reserve until another weapon has had time to attack, or can be vectored to another part of the engagement zone after completing one effective attack.

One way of using the A-10, which has been practised to the limited extent possible in peacetime, is 'ground loiter', a technique otherwise confined to the Harrier. If the A-10s are required to wait near the battle for any extended period, they can alight easily on a good stretch of road – and Germany's autobahns are the best in the world – and wait for a call to action. The APU keeps all the systems running while using a minimal amount of fuel, so the aircraft can start engines and take off at shorter notice than any other type.

The A-10 is the only weapon which offers this sort of performance without sacrificing the full mobility of airpower; this is one of the factors which distinguishes the A-10 from the tank-killing helicopter. The helicopter is slow and short-legged, and the commander at the scene is, for practical purposes, limited to the helicopter force in his immediate vicinity. The available helicopter resources

Below: An A-10 of the 57th TTW, now the 57th Fighter Weapons Wing, in one of the camouflage schemes evaluated during the JAWS (Joint Attack Weapons Systems) trials held at Fort Hunter Liggett, California, in November 1977. New tactics were tested against a variety of threats.

have to be spread out along the entire battle line, so the numbers available at any one spot will not be large enough to mount a strong counterattack. The A-10, however, is available for rapid reinforcement at any point.

Another attribute of the A-10 versus the helicopter is the ability of the faster fixed-wing aircraft to survive at close quarters with enemy SAM and AAA units. The helicopter is, essentially, an ambush weapon, unparalleled in its ability to find and exploit cover and attack from concealment. Its limitation is that it is most effective against the front and forward flanks of an advancing unit, and that it is unable to strike targets deep within the formation. Apart from the new AH-64, too, no helicopter has more than half the A-10's firepower, measured in effective anti-armour weaponry.

The tasks assigned to the A-10 in each phase of the battle reflect the type's strengths. In the early stages, as the advancing enemy spreads out through the van of the defences, the A-10s are available to respond quickly as advance ground forces engage the first enemy units. The ground forces delay the advance, and provide targeting information for effective attacks by A-10s.

Once the main force is engaged, the A-10 force can be used to provide 'fire-hose' CAS, a constant flow of sorties to the battle area which the commander can direct as necessary. The aircraft may support a unit in danger of being broken through, or exploit the brief opportunity offered by a new unit joining battle, and not yet fully deployed. In the case of a breakthrough, the A-10 force can be rapidly concentrated to slow the advancing force, attack the flanks of forces moving through the breach, and disrupt the movement of forces to the front. The last-named mission is not regarded as CAS, but is termed 'battlefield air interdiction', or BAI.

JAWS and JAAT

The way in which these operations are commanded and controlled is unique. The A-10 was the first TAC aircraft designed to work in such close proximity to hostile armoured forces, and the first which would be so closely integrated with the battle on the ground. It was in early 1977 that USAF and US Army officers began to discuss a common problem: that it was clearly wasteful and dangerous to confront an armoured attack in increments, each service sending in its own systems independently. The discussions led to the development of a concept called JAWS (joint attack weapons systems), in which the strong and weak points of the helicopter, artillery and the A-10 would be blended into a single system. Early trials took place at Fort Benning, Georgia, in September 1977, followed two months later by a full-scale JAWS exercise at Fort Hunter Liggett, California.

The JAWS trials were highly successful. The A-10's main task was to shoot tanks. Freed from that major burden, the Cobra helicopters concentrated on attacking the air defence systems, using the highest possible degree of concealment and the longest possible stand-off ranges. The presence of two airborne threats, with completely different speed and manoeuvrability characteristics, confused the air defence operators. A helicopter popping out of cover might be about to attack; the Shilka operator would traverse his turret and lock on, and the helicopter would promptly drop back behind the treeline, having simply intended to decoy the gunner away from an attacking A-10. Safe separation was assured by a simple rule of thumb: the attack helicopters held the airspace from the ground to the treetops, and the space above belonged to the A-10.

To the A-10 pilot, racing at low level with no overview of the battlefield, the presence and alignment of helicopters were always a clue to the presence of tanks over the hill. The helicopters would launch their first attack on the air-defence units as the A-10s passed them on their way in; then, as the A-10s left the scene, the gun and missile systems engaged the aircraft, betraying their positions for a second attack.

Once the scores were added up, it was found that the Cobras and A-10s working together had killed three to four times as many targets as had been hit in previous exercises by similar forces working separately. The vulnerability of both types was also greatly reduced. A Joint Air Attack Team (JAAT) manual was prepared, and the techniques developed in the JAWS exercises were written into regular A-10 operations.

Above left: The mottled paint schemes used for the JAWS tests were applied to every part of the aircraft, and were varied from day to day to match weather and terrain conditions.

Above: Following the JAWS trials, a 57th FWW A-10 in mottled camouflage was deployed to Ramstein AB, Germany, to participate in evaluation of infrared Maverick performance.

Good forward air control (FAC) – observation of battlefield targets, and the assignment of targets to different air assets – is crucial to successful JAAT operations. The A-10s and helicopters work within a common FAC structure, but tactics are not rigid. One important reason for flexibility, besides the fact that it leaves room for individual initiative, is that easy and reliable communications are not to be expected in the face of intense hostile jamming. Moreover, the A-10 pilots, in manual terrain-following flight en route to the battle area, have no time to take down attack instructions in exhaustive detail.

Instead, the JAAT philosophy stresses the importance of frequent joint practice and training sessions involving A-10s and helicopters, so that the A-10 pilots learn to fill their role in the JAAT with a minimum of briefing and only a few moments of communication with the FAC. The USAF's FAC aircraft, with their long endurance, are important in maintaining an overview of the action, and act as the 'traffic police', directing the A-10s to the starting points for their attack runs. Immediately before entering the target area, the A-10 pilots receive a last update from a front-line FAC operating from a helicopter, jeep or armoured personnel carrier.

The A-10 mission in Central Europe is highly demanding, and commanders say that even an experienced A-10 pilot transferred from the US will take at least a year to understand the mission completely. The need to comprehend the command and control system along an extended stretch of the front, possibly involving British, Dutch, Belgian and German forces, is added to the demands of the mission itself. In Europe, the A-10 pilots fly and train for a high-threat environment. In an engagement, they will jink constantly to throw off the defensive systems, and will pull more than 7g positive and 2.5-3g negative in the process. With its combination of long endurance and heavy armament, together with high sortie rates, the A-10 can spend far more time in combat than any other aircraft. The European A-10 force has a higher ratio of pilots to aircraft (28 pilots per 18-aircraft squadron) than the TAC average, because the ability of the aircraft would otherwise be limited by sheer pilot fatigue.

Training for Europe

Training is intensive. The new arrival is introduced to two-ship formation flying at progressively lower altitudes, and, when operating from the FOLs, the pilots simulate wartime sorties rates, flying two or three missions a day. Practice with an Aggressor unit also takes place regularly. In the 1982 fiscal year, the European A-10s alone accounted for 24 per cent of all the flying hours in US Air Forces Europe, and more hours than that of the next two wings combined. With the reduction of the perceived threat in Central Europe during the early 1990s, however, the total number of A-10s deployed in the theatre are likely to be greatly reduced.

Ugly and aggressive, the Warthog has a talent for arousing strong feelings. It certainly lacks the Lamborghini glamour of the F-16, or the puissant grace of the Eagle. Ground troops like the Warthog, possibly because it is the only TAC aircraft that will never be chasing MiG-23s five miles above their heads while the T-72s are running over their toes. An 81st TFW pilot summed up the A-10 pilots' attitudes: "Fighter pilots used to be short guys with big wristwatches and little airplanes who stayed far above the conflict. Warthog jockeys have little wristwatches and big airplanes, and go looking for a fight."

Below: An A-10 in JAWS markings outside its aircraft shelter at Ramstein AB. Testing of IIR missiles concentrated on performance in bad weather and battlefield smoke.

Above: During the JAWS trials, no live ammunition or missiles were fired, but data links to the range instrumentation system facilitated precise analysis of the results.

A FAC variant

While the two-seat variations on the A-10 theme failed to attain quantity production, the standard single-seat A-10A has provided the basis for one other version, specifically the OA-10A which made its debut in the late 1980s and which, as noted elsewhere, serves with elements of Tactical Air Command, Pacific Air Forces and the Air National Guard in modest quantities.

As the designation implies, it is more concerned with the observation mission, for it serves as a mount for airborne forward air controllers, even though it does retain the formidable attack capability of the baseline A-10A from which it stems. In fact, apart from the addition of an 'O' prefix to the designation of somewhere in the region of 60 aircraft, it is fundamentally unchanged and one would be hard pushed to differentiate between an A-10A and an OA-10A if examples of each sub-type were parked adjacent to each other on a flight line.

However, the different demands of the FAC mission are reflected in different training programmes and procedures. Since FAC duty basically entails co-ordinating the activities of warplanes engaged in close air support, including the identification and marking of targets, it follows that very different skills are needed in imparting the relevant information to attacking pilots. They, obviously, have plenty to think about as they run in to attack, so timely and accurate advice is essential if one is to avoid running the risk of a 'friendly fire' incident, especially when working an area in which friend and foe are in uncomfortably close proximity. For all that, tragic mistakes can occur in the 'heat of battle', as the recent Gulf war showed.

Glossary and abbreviations

AAA Anti-aircraft artillery, or all tube AA weapons. Usually spoken as "triple-A"
AB Air Base (USAF base outside USA)
AD Air Division (TAC formation)
AF Air Force (USAF formation)
AFB Air Force Base
AGM-US designation prefix for any air-to-ground missile
AIM-US designation prefix for any air-to-air missile
ALQ-US designation prefix for any active countermeasures equipment
ALR-US designation prefix for any radar-warning receiver
API Armour-piercing incendiary (ammunition)
APU Auxiliary power unit
BAI Battlefield air interdiction
BPR Bypass ratio
Bunt Wings-level, negative-g entry into a dive
Bypass ratio Ratio of the total airflow through a turbofan engine to that passing through the core section
CAS Close air support
CBU-US designation prefix for a cluster-bomb unit
COIN Counter-insurgency
CRT Cathode-ray tube (computer/TV-type display screen)
DT & E Development, test and evaluation
ECM Electronic countermeasures
EW Electronic warfare
FAC Forward air control, or forward air controller
Flir Forward-looking infra-red
FOD Foreign-object damage
FOL Forward operating location
FWW Fighter Weapons Wing (Nellis-based TAC unit)
GBU-US designation prefix for an unpowered guided bomb system
GPWS Ground-proximity warning system
HEI High explosive incendiary (ammunition)
HUD Head-up display
INS Inertial navigation system
In-weather Conditions of zero effective visibility due to cloud or rain. Term mainly used in connection with low-level flight or attack
JAAT Joint Air Attack Team
JAWS Joint Attack Weapons Systems
JTF Joint Test Force
Lantirn Low-Altitude Navigation, and Targeting by Infra-Red at Night
Lock-on The action of a missile or other system maintaining contact with a target using its own sensors
Manual reversion Provision for a control surface to be moved by human force alone in the event of power failure
N/AW Night/adverse-weather
Pk Kill probability of a weapon, expressed as a decimal of 1. Single-shot pK of 0.5 means that one round in two will kill the target
RFP Request for proposals
RWR Radar-warning receiver
SA-Nato-assigned designation to prefix for Soviet surface-to-air missile system, including all ground equipment
TAC Tactical Air Command
TFG Tactical Fighter Group (ANG or AFRES formation only)
TFR Terrain-following radar
TFS Tactical Fighter Squadron (nominal strength 18 aircraft)
TFTS Tactical Fighter Training Squadron
TFTW Tactical Fighter Training Wing
TFW Tactical Fighter Wing (normally, four TFS)
TFWC Tactical Fighter Weapons Center, Nellis AFB
TP Target Practice (ammunition)

Specifications

Fairchild A-10A

			Definition	Northrop YA-9A
Dimensions	Wing span	57ft 6in/17.53m		58ft/17.67m
	Length overall	53ft 4in/16.26m		56ft 6in/17.22m
	Height overall	14ft 8in/4.47m		16ft 11in/5.16m
	Wing area	506sq ft/47.01m²		580sq ft/53.9m²
Powerplant		Two GE TF34-GE-100A		Two Avco-Lycoming YF102-LD-100
	Thrust (each)	9,065lb/40.3kN		7,500lb/33.3kN
	Bypass ratio	6.2:1		
Weights	Operating empty	24,959lb/11,321kg	Pilot, oxygen, unusable fuel and oil, gun and six pylons	
	Basic design weight	30,384lb/13,782kg	Maximum weight at 7.33 g	
	Internal fuel	10,700lb/4,853kg		
	Max external load	16,000lb/7,250kg		
Take-off weights	Clean			26,000lb/11,800kg
	Maximum	50,000lb/22,680kg		42,000lb/1,905kg
	CAS mission	47,094lb/21,362kg	18 565lb (256kg) Mk 82 bombs, 750 rounds of ammunition and full internal fuel	
	Anti-armour mission	42,071lb/19,083kg	Six Mavericks on triple launchers, 1,174 rounds of ammunition, ALQ-119, 480 flare/chaff cartridges and full internal fuel	
	Ferry	49,774lb/22,577kg	Full internal fuel and three 600 US gal (2,271lit) external tanks	
Performance	Never-exceed speed	450kt/834km/h		390kt/723km/h
	Max level speed at sea level, clean	381kt/706km/h		
	Combat speed at 5,000ft (1525m) with six Mk 82 bombs	380kt/704km/h		
	Cruising speed at sea level	300kt/555km/h		270kt/500km/h
	Sea-level rate of climb at design weight	6,000ft/min/1,828m/min		
	Service ceiling	45,000ft/13715m		
Combat radii	Anti-armour configuration, 30min combat, 40nm (74km) sea-level penetration and exit	252nm/467km		250nm (463km) with 2hr loiter
	CAS configuration, 1.88hr single-engine loiter at 5,000ft (1525m), 10min combat	250nm/463km		
	Ferry range, 50kt (93km) headwinds, 20min reserve	2,240nm/4,148km		

Deployment as at mid-1991

US-based Operators

Tactical Air Command
Direct Reporting Units 57th FWW, Nellis AFB, Nevada ('WA') (A-10 FWS, 422nd TES)
Tactical Air Warfare Center, Eglin AFB, Florida ('OT') (4485th TS)
Ninth Air Force, Shaw AFB, South Carolina 23rd TFW, England AFB, Louisiana ('EL') (74th, 75th, 76th TFS)
354th TFW, Myrtle Beach AFB, South Carolina ('MB') (353rd, 355th 356th TFS)
Twelfth Air Force, Bergstrom AFB, Texas 836th Air Division, Davis-Monthan AFB, Arizona
355th TTW, Davis-Monthan AFB, Arizona ('DM') (333rd, 357th, 358th TFTS)
602nd TACW, Davis-Monthan AFB, Arizona ('NF') (23rd TASS)

Air Force Systems Command
Munitions Systems Division, Eglin AFB, Florida ('ET') (3246th TW/3247th TS)
Air Force Flight Test Center, Edwards AFB, California ('ED') (6513th TS)

Air Force Logistics Command
Sacramento Air Logistics Center, McClellan AFB, California (occasional trials and depot level repair)

Air National Guard
103rd TASS/111th TASG, Willow Grove NAS, Pennsylvania ('PA')
104th TFS/175th TFG, Baltimore-Martin Airport, Maryland ('MD')
118th TFS/103rd TFG, Bradley Field, Connecticut ('CT')
131st TFS/104th TFG, Barnes Airport, Massachusetts ('MA')
176th TFS/128th TFW, Truax Field, Wisconsin ('WI')

Air Force Reserve
Tenth Air Force, Bergstrom AFB, Texas 442nd TFW, Richards-Gebaur AFB, Missouri ('KC') (303rd TFS)
930th TFG, Grissom AFB, Indiana ('IN') (45th TFS)
917th TFW, Barksdale AFB, Louisiana ('BD') (46th TFTS, 47th TFS)
926th TFG, New Orleans NAS, Louisiana ('NO') (760th TFS)

Overseas-based Operators

United States Air Forces in Europe
Third Air Force, RAF Mildenhall, England 10th TFW, RAF Alconbury, England ('AR') (509th, 511th TFS)
(Det.3, Ahlhorn, Germany)
81st TFW, RAF Bentwaters, England ('WR') (78th*, 91st*, 92nd, 510th TFS)
(Det.1, Sembach, Germany)
(Det.2, Leipheim, Germany)
(Det.4, Norvenich, Germany)
* = located at RAF Woodbridge

Pacific Air Forces
Seventh Air Force, Osan AB, South Korea 5th TACG, Suwon AB South Korea ('SU') (19th TASS)
Eleventh Air Force, Elmendorf AFB, Alaska 343rd TFW, Eielson AFB, Alaska ('AK') (18th TFS)